ENDORSEMENTS

"Lily's passion for helping others heal radiates throughout the book. Her words are not just written; they are carefully crafted to uplift, to inspire, and to guide. The book encourages readers to embrace their own stories, confront their traumas and, most importantly, to believe in the possibility of healing".... Julie

"This is a must read book for those who want to heal childhood trauma or wounds from their past. Many people struggle with wounds that hold them back from becoming their true, healed selves. This book will help you identify the past hurts and teach you how to holistically heal them. This is a book that will teach you skills to live in harmony with yourself emotionally, physically, and mentally".... Justin

"Lily's storytelling is a masterful blend of personal narrative and expert advice. She candidly shares her own experiences with trauma, inviting readers into her world with remarkable authenticity. Her openness and honesty create an immediate connection, making the reader feel understood and supported on their own path to healing".... Alma

"Rise Up and Heal" is a powerful testament to the human spirit's capacity for transformation and renewal. Lily's remarkable storytelling and her dedication to helping others heal make this book a must-read for anyone seeking to rise above the shadows of trauma and rediscover their inner strength".... Damary

Rise Up and Heal

How to Use Your Inner Gifts to Turn Your Pain into Your Testimony and Inspire Others to Heal from the Inside Out

Lily Robinson

Rise Up and Heal © 2023 by Lily Robinson. All rights reserved.

Published by Lily Robinson
Morgan Hill CA 95037

All rights reserved. This book contains material protected under international and federal copyright laws and treaties. Any unauthorized reprint or use of this material is prohibited. No part of this book may be reproduced or transmitted in any form or by any means, electronic or mechanical, including photocopying, recording, or by any information storage and retrieval system, without express written permission from the author.

Identifiers:

LCCN: 2023916482
ISBN: 979-8-218-27216-6 (paperback)
ISBN: 979-8-218-27217-3 (hardback)
ISBN: 979-8-218-27218-0 (ebook)

Available in paperback, hardback, e-book, and audiobook

All Scripture quotations, unless otherwise indicated, are taken from the Holy Bible, New International Version®, NIV®. Copyright © 1973, 1978, 1984 by Biblica, Inc.™ Used by permission. All rights reserved worldwide.

Any Internet addresses (websites, blogs, etc.) and telephone numbers printed in this book are offered as a resource. They are not intended in any way to be or imply an endorsement by the Author, nor does the Author vouch for the content of these sites and numbers for the life of this book.

Some names and identifying details have been changed to protect the privacy of individuals.

DEDICATION

I dedicate this book to my children.

I also dedicate it to all the women who have experienced childhood trauma and emotional trauma at some point in their lives and to all the men and women who are determined to Rise Up and Heal so that they can become the best version of themselves.

CONTENTS

Endorsements i

Dedication v

Introduction xi
   When you find your inner power,
     you can heal and set yourself free. xi

Part I: Your Inner Gifts

Chapter 1: Your Body 3
   You Are What You Eat 9
   The Importance of Restful Sleep. 15

Chapter 2: Your Mind. 18

Chapter 3: Your Soul and Spirit. 22

Chapter 4: Your Intuition 25

Part II: Healing Truths and the Human Body's Ability to Restore Itself

Chapter 5: The Body's Ability to Restore Itself.... 35
    Breathing Exercises and Our Bodies 37
    The Power of Our Gut Microbiome 41
    Your Immune System..................... 43

Chapter 6: Nutrition....................... 46

Chapter 7: Meditation...................... 55

Part III: Healing Stories

Chapter 8: Grandma....................... 61
    Generational Curses and Generational Blessings ... 61
    Grandpa's Gambling..................... 69
    Emotional Pain Has Physical Consequences ... 73

Chapter 9: Ana........................... 81
    A Traumatic Childhood 81
    Addictions, Mental Health, Childhood Trauma
        and the Problems These Issues Bring
        When We Don't Heal from Them 110

The Story of Ana and John and
  How Their Childhood Traumas Negatively
  Impacted Their Marriage. 114
Hurt People, Addictions, and Codependency. . . 152
Sexual Abuse, Sexual Molestation, and
  Sexual Harassment 159

Chapter 10: Miriam 175
Toxic Relationships 175
Narcissism and Why Men Are More Likely
  to Have It vs. Women 190
Genetic Differences in Men vs. Women 196

PART IV: YOUR NEXT STEPS

Chapter 11: Finding Your Inner Power. 205
Do the Mirror Work 205
The Story of the Golden Buddha 208

Acknowledgments. 213
Notes 215
About the Author 227

INTRODUCTION

WHEN YOU FIND YOUR INNER POWER,
YOU CAN HEAL AND SET YOURSELF FREE.

When bad things happen to good people, how do we respond? We've all have asked ourselves this question many times, yet we still don't have the answer.

Our society has created an environment of confusion, deep insecurities, trauma, ego, control, narcissism, war within ourselves, and lack of love. In return, we have to deal with toxic behaviors and illnesses that can be cured by healing our emotional trauma. Realizing this led me to ask questions about my own trauma:

- How do we heal from the pain and trauma we face in life?

- How do we heal our bodies from all the trapped energy and emotions that hurt us deeply?
- How can we learn techniques that teach us how to heal our psychological traumas?
- How can we become fully healthy and free?

If we take responsibility for our actions and make ourselves vulnerable, this type of healing is within our reach. Responsibility and awareness are the foundations to changing anything. First, we need to become aware of what is hurting us and what is blocking our potential, and then we need to take responsibility for our healing journey.

Here are some examples of trauma that greatly affect our physical health:

- Emotional abuse in familial or romantic relationships
- Betrayal
- Grief from losing a loved one or a close relationship
- Trauma that results from unmet needs and unmet expectations
- Different types of child abuse, such as physical, emotional, sexual abuse

How do we heal from emotional abuse? How can a child heal from loosing a parent a a young age? How can a mother who lost her child due to an illness or a tragic accident heal? Or how can a wife who lost her husband learn to heal? How do we heal from trauma and unmet needs or unmet expectations? How do we heal our childhood traumas? How do we, as humans, heal from all the pain and trauma we go through in life?

We try to run with life in hopes that things will get better. We take on so many responsibilities, and many of us take on responsibilities that do not even belong to us. We are not supposed to carry those responsibilities. We deal with coping mechanisms that cause us to carry more responsibilities than what actually belong to us. As we go through life, we keep adding burden after burden without even noticing how all of that affects our bodies, minds, and souls. It affects us in a very negative way.

I want to talk about a very serious trauma that happens to many people, and unfortunately, not a lot of people talk about it. Many of us don't pay attention to it, and it's very important to recognize and work on, if we want to fully heal our emotional traumas.

Childhood abandonment is a big and serious emotional trauma that many of us carry. I'm not just talking about abandonment due to a father or mother passing away or not being there physically. I'm talking about not being present. You can also abandon and emotionally damage your child by not being present.

Being physically or emotionally absent can create deep wounds in a child's inner spirit, in their emotions, and even impair the development of their brain. It creates fear, insecurities, and emotional traumas that are hard to heal as an adult.

According to a Harvard University briefing, the Center on the Developing Child says, "Babies' brains require stable, caring, interactive relationships with adults—any way or any place they can be provided will benefit healthy brain development."[1] They also say that "toxic stress damages developing brain architecture, which can lead to lifelong problems in learning, behavior, and physical and mental health."[2] They also say that "the basic principles of neuroscience indicate that early preventive intervention will be more efficient and produce more favorable outcomes than remediation later in life."[3]

Experts at healthline.com say that "when it comes to child development, it's been said that the most crucial milestones in a kid's life occur by the age of 7. In fact, the great Greek philosopher Aristotle once said, 'Give me a child until he is 7 and I will show you the man.'"[4]

This is a strong statement, and I strongly believe it's true. It is not hard to believe that what happens in a child's brain and emotional well-being during the first seven years will either have a negative or positive impact in his life as an adult and it will determine his ability to face life's challenges.

If the child has a foundation that includes love, self-confidence, and the ability to self-regulate his emotions, then he will be better prepared to handle any difficult challenge that he may face in his life.

We all face challenges in life, and the question is not if or when we will face challenges. The question is, are we willing to rise up from life's challenges with courage, love, and wisdom?

It makes me very sad to see that there are many people who were raised in fear and with insecurities that stem from emotional abuse and neglect by their parents. Their hearts and souls were crushed from an early age, and when they become adults, they are not able to regulate their emotions. They become wounded adults who are full of fears, insecurities, toxic mechanisms, and deep childhood trauma.

This is why it is crucial that we as parents or legal guardians are aware of the importance of being present, caring, loving, protective, and nurturing toward our children. It is the environment we create that will determine what kind of human beings we raise.

Frederick Douglass once said, "It is easier to build strong children than to repair broken men."[5]

When we build strong and confident children, they can maneuver in life as adults in a much healthier way. However, children who do not get to experience a loving upbringing grow up to be adults with skewed perceptions of love and happiness. It is harder to heal and repair all the broken pieces as an adult for several reasons:

- The brokenness from childhood often feels permanent.
- It is challenging to change ingrained behaviors as adults.
- Child neglect or emotional abandonment is extremely harmful to the brain.
- The healing process is long and intense; it won't happen overnight.

- It takes an intensive amount of work (through therapy or personal development) to become confident and whole.

One of the reasons all these things are true is because emotional abuse is very hard to identify. It can take many years to pinpoint and identify emotional abuse, but once you isolate the source, a huge weight lifts from your shoulders, and you start feeling free and empowered to begin your healing journey.

Some of us probably had healthy childhoods, but we could also develop emotional trauma as we face challenges in life.

Little by little and unaware of it, we end up being buried in pain, frustration, resentment, disappointments, and burdens that drag us down into the pit of emotional and psychological trauma.

These emotional burdens take away our abilities to function as healthy adults. Our bodies were not designed for that. When we carry emotional pain, disappointments, and resentment, our bodies and souls store negative energy, and in return, our bodies and souls get sick and stuck in toxic patterns.

God created us to be in tune with our hearts and souls. When we can reach our higher selves (the healthy us inside and out), we can see and understand the true purpose each of us have in life. We need to get in tune with ourselves if we want to rise up and heal. We need to work on finding our inner peace, even if our current circumstances have not fully changed.

We need to remind ourselves that healing is a journey. It takes time. As we start making small changes, we will see that we can think more clear, and we can make better and wiser decisions in our lives.

When we are in tune with ourselves, we are able to rise up and be at peace within ourselves, even if our circumstances haven't fully changed. Things will change over time and you will see that the healing journey you went through was worth it. Just be patient and kind to yourself.

When bad things happen to us, fear will always try to derail us, and then we are going to start doubting ourselves. It's in our human nature to start analyzing what went wrong. We start feeling confused and frustrated, wondering what went wrong. This confusion can discourage us, causing us to resent our creator, ourselves, and those around us, ultimately leading us to doubt our journeys. We need to find a way to turn this negativity into a feeling of empowerment, joy, hope, and wholeness.

How do we switch from feeling discouraged and emotionally drained to feeling empowered, joyful, hopeful, and emotionally healed? Life knows how to throw the biggest and most hurtful curveballs at us. It feels like a gut punch.

Life often throws the most painful curveballs at us, but I believe we can get up stronger. I personally know we can use our pain and turn it into a story of healing and inspiration that brings healing and hope to others. This is the reason I wrote this book—I believe you have the power to find your emotional, spiritual, and physical healing. It won't always be easy because I'll ask you questions that require you to dig deep into your soul. However, in the end, you will receive infinite encouragement to start your healing journey. If I can do it, you can do it too! Believe you can and you will.

If I can help bring emotional, spiritual and physical healing to others, I've served my purpose in this world.

With this book, my goal is to bring awareness and to cause you to ask yourself questions that will help you dig deep into your soul and feel encouraged to start your healing journey.

PART I
Your Inner Gifts

You are already equipped with
what you need to heal yourself.

1

YOUR BODY

We have the power within ourselves to rise up and transform our pain into power and joy. Our stories of transformation will also bring healing to others. God created us and gave us the power to heal ourselves. Healing is certainly not an easy process but it's worth it. It is worth it, when you finally connect with that inner light that exists inside of you.

Let me share a little bit about what the Bible says in regards to us healing ourselves and rewiring our minds. According to the Bible, we were created in God's image, therefore we have God's blueprint. I'm not going to go deep into it, but I will share just a little bit of what I understand and how I view it. According to the Bible, we have the ability to heal ourselves.

Genesis 1:26–27 says:

"Then God said, 'Let us make mankind in our image, in our likeness, so that they may rule over the fish in the sea and the birds in the sky, over the livestock and all the wild animals, and over all the creatures that move along the ground.' So God created mankind in his own image, in the image of God he created them; male and female he created them."

John 14:20–21 says:

"On that day you will realize that I am in my Father, and you are in me, and I am in you. Whoever has my commands and keeps them is the one who loves me. The one who loves me will be loved by my Father, and I too will love them and show myself to them."

John 14:25–27 says:

"'All this I have spoken while still with you. But the Advocate, the Holy Spirit, whom the Father will send in my name, will teach you all things and will remind you of everything I have said to you. Peace I leave with you; my peace I give you. I do not give to you as the world gives. Do not let your hearts be troubled and do not be afraid.'"

Mark 9:23 says:

"'If you can?' said Jesus. 'Everything is possible for one who believes.'"

Mark 11:24 says:

"'Therefore I tell you, whatever you ask for in prayer, believe that you have received it, and it will yours.'"

Romans 12:2-3 says:

"Do not conform to the pattern of this world, but be transformed by the renewing of your mind. Then you will be able to test and approve what God's will is— his good, pleasing and perfect will."

All these words are powerful and they clearly show our connection to our creator and how amazing our blueprint is. It shows us who we are as his creation. God's love and Spirit is within us. His Spirit will teach usb and will guide us with wisdom if we allow him.

According to his words, we have the power to heal ourselves. We have the power to renew our minds.

We need to believe that we can, and we need to believe in our journeys. Our bodies are perishable, but our souls are eternal. If we can understand our journeys and be at peace within, no matter what happens to us, we will be okay and we will come to terms with our journeys.

Every journey has a purpose. We are not perfect, but it all makes perfect sense. Life is beautiful, and our purpose as human beings is a journey and a miracle in itself.

We are beautiful beings who have many spiritual gifts, and one of these gifts is the ability to change our sorrow into joy. The beauty of life is when we change our mess into a message. When we discover we have the power to be at peace within ourselves and in acceptance of our journeys, we can bring hope to others. How powerful is that!? Yes, that's who we are. We are powerful.

Please understand we are still going to have problems because we are only human, but it is our mindsets that will give us different outcomes and a new perspective in life. This perspective is what I hope to show you throughout this book. If you are open to receive the message, you can discover your inner power on your way to healing yourself spiritually, emotionally, and physically.

We were created with the ability to transform our lives, and we constantly evolve even when we don't know it or see it. Listen to that small voice that guides you, and you will find your path. You will see with clarity who you are truly meant to be.

Each of us have a purpose, and that purpose is worth living no matter what we go through in life. Make sure you are truly living and not just going through the motions. Sometimes we do this because we are waiting for change to find us; however, that is not how transformation works. Don't let fear paralyze you into living in your trauma for too long.

Our hearts, spirits, and minds are the most beautiful gifts we receive as human beings. The power within us lives in our minds, spirits, and hearts. All we need to do is tap into our intuition and exercise it. Ask God for wisdom. The more we tune into it, the more we develop it.

We can do this through prayer and meditation. As we connect with God, we should ask Him important questions that lead us to powerful answers. Throughout this process, you will come to accept God's love and timing, leading you to also accept who you are, who you were truly meant to be. It requires a great deal of trust and honesty to start this journey with God, but He will help you. His wisdom and love will nourish your body and soul, as you learn to surrender. As you learn to live in the present moment. As you learn to let go of what no longer serves you.

When we tune into our intuition, we discover our powerful gifts. This discovery comes from God's perfect blueprint for us, and it enables us to make a difference in people's lives and everywhere we go. We were put in this world to be love and to give love, to make a positive impact. This ability to have compassion for yourself and others will take you far in your journey to find inner peace and, ultimately, to find your true, healed self.

Our intuition is the magic within us. If we don't tap into this power, we lose the wisdom within us. We lose the connection with our creator. It requires us to be disciplined with our bodies, minds, and souls. It requires us to be willing and vulnerable, opening ourselves up to reliving traumas that have forged a path of pain for years.

God gives us the wisdom and perseverance we need to survive our emotional traumas so we can heal. He shows us the path to accepting ourselves as we allow the process of our journeys to unfold.

It is important that we nourish our Bodies, Minds, and Spirits with gentleness. It all starts with being intentional and mindful.

You Are What You Eat

Let's talk about our Bodies, Minds, and Spirits, how it all works, and how important it is to nourish them with gentleness. It is important to be intentional in everything we do and how we process our thoughts and emotions. Let's start with our bodies…

For our bodies to be healthy and functional, we need to start with the food we eat. Remember the old adage: you are what you eat. It is very important to eat healthy, clean, and fresh organic foods if possible. Processed foods have no nutrition and will not nurture your body, so I recommend staying away from those as often as possible.

The food we eat will either help us heal or make our bodies ill. Nowadays, many of us have sensitivities or resistances to some foods. Food is not quite the same as it was when we were children; it is more processed now and has fewer nutrients. This unfortunate shift in our food culture makes us more prone to illnesses and other issues.

When you focus on your personal health, your body will automatically tell you what hurts it or heals it. Pay attention to how your food makes you feel—this is one productive way you can be intentional about caring for your body. If you are serious about making changes in your nutrition, one thing you can do is keep a food journal that includes a section about how each meal or snack made you feel. Make note of anything that has a negative effect on your mood or your body so you can remember to stay away from that later.

For example, I decided to stay away from coffee because I was having trouble sleeping. It also made me feel anxious, and I realized later the caffeine had depleted me of my vitamins. This was a huge problem for me because I am super passionate about taking my vitamins—not to mention, they can be expensive, so the coffee was hurting me in many ways. When I noticed these negative side effects, I knew I had to make a change.

This change was not easy for me to make.

Here I am, super passionate about my healthy and expensive vitamins, thinking I am healthy and I am nourishing my body very well. As it turned out, not really, because when I noticed all the side effects I had, due to my "delicious" coffee, I had to make a change.

I would religiously prepare my coffee every morning, making a ritual out of it. Grinding my organic coffee beans every morning, I would pour it into my French press, then I would froth organic whole milk and use a little bit of organic honey. I would sit down and enjoy every sip of it with excitement, feeling so proud of myself. At night, I would go to sleep thinking about my perfect morning coffee I planned to make the next day.

We all do it. If I ever heard anyone say, "I don't drink coffee," I would wonder how in the world, could they go through their day without coffee. I might say, "You just haven't tried my coffee." That's how addicted I was to my coffee, not even knowing how much it affected my health.

I remember when I started wondering about my coffee and how often I had to use the restroom. My thoughts would go to: What if my coffee is the reason why my heart pumps really fast, and what if the reason I feel restless and anxious has to do with my coffee? What if my morning coffee is messing with my sleep? At the time, I was getting up to use the bathroom about two to three times at night, and I also had joint pain and acid reflux. These realizations led to asking myself more questions.

First, I read more about the effects coffee has on the body, and learning it was depleting my body of vitamins was a hard pill to swallow. As I previously mentioned, I was wasting money taking my expensive vitamins if my coffee addiction was negating their benefits.

Coffee can also make your body acidic, which is never a good thing for your health. Being slightly acidic might not be a detriment to your health, but getting too out-of-balance forces your kidneys and lungs to work much harder to remove the excess acid. This imbalance can often lead to the following changes in your health:[6]

- Rapid and shallow breathing
- Confusion
- Fatigue
- Headache

- Sleepiness
- Lack of appetite
- Increased heart rate
- Breath that smells fruity (sign of diabetic acidosis)

If you start to notice any of these symptoms, I highly recommend you seek medical attention to get your body back in balance first. For me, I had a suspicion that my coffee consumption was what was causing problems, so I started looking for healthy alternatives to coffee.

I switched to chai latte with ashwagandha, turmeric, probiotics, and mushrooms, which have a lot of great benefits for your health. Every morning, I make it with organic coconut milk. It is so yummy, frothy, and delicious. I love it! and there is no need for me to compromise my health.

I also do the same thing with Yerba mate. Yerba mate is like green tea, but it doesn't affect my nervous system. It gives me natural energy, and it's loaded with vitamins, minerals, and antioxidants.

It was a little hard when I made the switch at first, but I started noticing how my body changed for the better. I didn't have to go to the bathroom often during the day, and I could sleep at night without having to get up several times.

I enjoyed more benefits too: I felt calmer during the day, I had more energy, I felt more focused, and my acid reflux went away. I couldn't believe my morning coffee was making me sick!

It was a simple change, but it made a huge difference in my health. Now, please know that I still have my yummy warm cup of ritual every morning. You don't have to sacrifice what you love; you just modify it. My morning ritual is still there, but now it's a healthy cup of goodness.

Here's my question for you:

What is it that you may need to take a break from or let go of? Is it your cup of coffee, gluten, sugar, processed foods, nicotine, or alcohol? Or is there something else making your body sick? If you're not sure what it is about your nutrition that's making you sick, you can try experimenting with eliminating one thing at a time. Go back to that journal I recommended earlier and keep track of how it changes your health.

The Importance of Restful Sleep

Sleep is critical for helping our minds and bodies reset for the next day. Getting restful sleep will allow us to think clearly, and in return, we make better decisions in our day-to- day tasks. This has the ability to empower you with the energy and focus you need to keep making healthy decisions every day.

Sleep also straightens our microbiome in our guts. The body resets and recovers during sleep. When the body and mind receive quality sleep, this helps the healthy bacteria to reproduce and fight bad bacteria. The more healthy bacteria we have in our guts, the healthier we will be. A healthy gut microbiome is basically your first brain, which communicates with the brains in our heads. Our brain can have trouble communicating with our gut microbiome if we have unhealthy sleeping patterns. Prioritize quality sleep, and you will start seeing small changes in your health.

Your body and brain are happier and more alert when you are rested. You can tackle any problems or stresses that come your way as you go through life. Stress is unavoidable, but it really matters how we manage it.

Quality sleep helps regulate your hormones. When you get quality sleep, this benefits your brain and body. We know now that our brains reset every time we sleep. This is how our brains process information and restore our bodies' ability to cope with everyday challenges. A lack of sleep can bring many health problems, such as anxiety, depression, mood swings, anger, weight gain, weak immune system, etc.

A study by sleepfoundation.org shares with us the health benefits of a restful sleep. There are many benefits, such as lower risk of diabetes and heart disease, healthy and steady body weight, mental stability, ability to make better decisions, and it reduces stress and anxiety.

Most adults need 7–8 hours of quality sleep every night.[7] Some people may find it beneficial with just six hours of sleep, and some will need more. Get to know your body and what makes it function at its best.

Children need more sleep than adults: teens will benefit from 8 to 10 hours of sleep. Elementary school kids will need 8–12 hours of sleep. Toddlers need 11–14 hours of sleep. Babies need 12–16 including naps. Newborn babies will need even more sleep: 14–17 hours every day.[8]

As you can see, sleep is very important, and it is more important that we prioritize quality sleep vs. quantity because oversleeping can also give you bad side effects.

When you oversleep, this brings physical side effects. According to WebMD, oversleeping can cause the body to have many health problems, such as heart disease, depression, diabetes, and even increased risk of death.[9]

In life, as with our health, it all comes down to balance. Balance is everything. I cannot overemphasize to love yourself enough to eat healthy, exercise, and prioritize quality sleep to live a happy and fulfilling life.

2

YOUR MIND

Your mind is connected to your body, and it works similarly to a software program powering a computer. Our bodies can't function if we don't have healthy brains. When we eat healthy foods, exercise, sleep restfully, and meditate, our brains, in return, protect us and help us think better.

Consider, for a moment, the time and money you put into your vehicle's maintenance. Without caring for your car regularly, it wouldn't operate well enough to take you where you need to go. Sometimes in our lives, we might not have enough money to pay for the premium-level service, and we notice a difference in the way it runs. Our brains work a lot like this; they need the higher-quality fuel to allow our bodies to function at their optimal level.

On top of that, your brain also consumes 20 percent of the nutrition you consume daily.[10] So, what do you think will happen to your brain if you're consistently giving it the lower-quality fuel? All the functions of your brain will suffer as a result.

But when you use the premium fuel for your brain, you might notice the following benefits:

- More stable energy
- Clearer thinking ability
- Healthier and brighter ideas
- Respect for your physical health
- Wiser decision-making skills
- Less anxious

When we are healthy on the inside, in return, we become healthy on the outside. We start seeing life differently than everyone else.

Unfortunately, the majority of people live their lives running from one task to another and eating junk food and not exercising. They also live with an incredible amount of stress, and they adopt that toxic lifestyle, thinking that it is normal because that is how they've been taught to live.

I am here to tell you that there is nothing normal about that way of living. You will burn out and become ill and depressed and will eventually die without learning your true purpose or discovering your true potential in life.

When we live our lives on high stress and eating unhealthy foods, our bodies don't have the same ability to respond to life's challenges with a healthy mindset. In return, we will make more mistakes. Our unhealthy patterns build up and we end up having a domino effect that not only hurt us but it also affect many other areas of our lives. When we eat unhealthy food and have unhealthy lifestyles, our brain and other organs in our bodies do not function properly.

A diet rich in antioxidants, vitamins, minerals, and healthy fatty acids will give your brain the right fuel so it functions better.[11] Some of the foods that are good for your brain include blueberries, salmon, leafy greens, walnuts, sardines, blackberries, and raspberries.[12] Omega-3 fatty acid supplements are also great for your brain if you are not able to get enough from fish and other sources.[13] In general, processed foods, refined white flours and pastas, processed cheeses and meats, alcohol, sugar, microwave popcorn, and fried foods create disfunction in your system and it deteriorates your brain cells.[14]

3

YOUR SOUL AND SPIRIT

When we tune into our intuition, we can hear that small voice inside of us. We all have it. That small voice is full of wisdom and love. The more we exercise it, the more wisdom we receive, and the more we learn to love and nurture ourselves. When we decide to be honest with ourselves and dig deep into our hearts, we can see the things that hold us back. Our souls and spirits will always guide us in the right direction. All we need to do is tune in, sit still, and listen.

Our spirits are always willing to help us grow, and they gently whisper in our ears what path to walk. God has given us the ability to connect with his wisdom through our spirits. Our spirits guide us and always show us what to do and how to become the best version of ourselves.

The Bible talks a lot about our souls and spirits. I will share a few of my favorite verses with you.

Our souls are eternal, and it is important to nurture them with good thoughts. I love this Bible verse in 3 John 1:2 that says, "Dear friend, I pray that you may enjoy good health and that all may go well with you, even as your soul prospers."

How amazing is that verse? I just love it when we get clear guidance from the Bible and it helps us live healthier lives. Matthew 16:26 says, "'What good will it be for someone to gain the whole world, yet forfeit their soul? Or what can anyone give in exchange for their soul?'"

Another amazing verse in Psalm 139:14 says, "I praise you because I am fearfully and wonderfully made; your works are wonderful, I know that full well."

1 Corinthians 15:44 says, "it is sown a natural body, it is raised a spiritual body. If there is a natural body, there is also a spiritual body."

I could share many more verses from the Bible and more information regarding our souls and spirits, but

I think I you got my point already. Our souls are eternal and our spirits influence our souls. This is why it is important for us humans to nurture our souls and spirits, because at the end of the day, whatever we do, they will give us the foundation for either an unhealthy or a healthy mind, body, and spirit and, ultimately, a healthy or unhealthy life. The choice is up to us.

4

YOUR INTUITION

Another term I like to use for "intuition" is a "third eye." We all hear that a lot, but I don't think that people understand it fully. Some of us don't want to even use that word because of religious beliefs. Let me share with you what I personally think it actually is.

Many people talk about our third eye being in the middle of our foreheads, and that our third eye give us intuition, telepathy, awareness, and much more. I personally believe our third eye are not between our eyes.

I believe the power from our third eye comes from the connectivity between our gut, heart, and mind. This connection is how our creator engineered the human body. The third eye reminds me of the trinity in the

Bible. The Father, the Son, and the Holy Spirit make up the biblical trinity, while our gut, heart, and mind makes up our biological trinity. When I say three in one, I mean our gut being #1 and our heart being #2 and our mind being #3. You are probably going to think, what? How could this be! It makes perfect sense to me.

I know that what I am saying may be a little hard to understand for some people. This is how I personally see it: our gut guides us and sends signals to our heart and brain. Then our heart drives us to take action on whatever decisions we make in life (some are good and some are bad). Then, our brain executes the directions of our heart and mind.

This is why it is very important to know yourself deeply so you can connect your heart, gut, and mind. This concept will help you strengthen your gut feeling. When your gut is healthy spiritually and physically, you will have better health and a much better intuition that will guide you and help you make wiser decisions in life. Our gut, heart, and mind are meant to be in harmony with each other so that our intuition can be working properly.

You know the gut feeling that we all talk about? This feeling is our third eye, and it is extremely important to our livelihood. This gut feeling radiates from the centers of our bodies, and it gives us intuition, telepathy, awareness, and much more.

When we are in tune with our gut, we can make wiser decisions in our lives. This wiser version of ourselves have the power to save our lives and even the lives of others. When we are in tune with ourselves, we are aware of our intuition in a mighty and powerful way.

You see, my friend, God created us all with incredible spiritual gifts and so much power. We are so much more than what our society has been trying to make us believe. Society has been shutting us down and has been making us feel like we have no power to heal ourselves from within. Step outside your limited beliefs. Rise up and empower yourself to become the healthiest and best version of yourself. Be present and ask God to help you develop your inner wisdom. Nurture your soul, mind and body!

Psalm 139:14 says, "I praise you because I am fearfully and wonderfully made; your works are wonderful, I know that full well."

That is the power that our creator designed us with. When we are in tune with our souls and spirits, the way God created us, our bodies in return can communicate perfectly with our souls. This is merely another way to say our intuition, our gut, or our "third eye."

We were meant to be in tune with our internal power, our soul, our spirit, and the wisdom our creator give us every day. Can our intuition be The Holy Spirit that the Bible talks about? I'll let you be the judge of that.

God created us with this amazing blueprint that gives us all the tools we need to tap into our divine wisdom. Don't believe the lies of society. Society is accustomed to giving us a diagnosis and we are constantly told that there is so much wrong with us and with our bodies, it's causing us to actually believe those lies. But here is the truth as I see it: we create the wrong when we don't nourish our Bodies, Minds, and Souls.

We create the wrong by allowing those lies to dictate how to live our lives. When we believe we are our childhood traumas, that's when we create the wrong. When we believe our fears and insecurities, that's when we create the wrong. When we believe a diagnosis given to us, that's when we create the wrong. When we try to be someone we are not, that's when we create the wrong. When we allow toxic people in our lives, when we allow toxic foods into our bodies, and when we adopt an unhealthy lifestyle, that's when we create the wrong. We create the wrong when we live disconnected from our true selves.

Cultivate your love for and belief in yourself. When you wake up every morning, thank your Creator and yourself for doing what you are doing. When you go to sleep at night, thank your Creator and yourself. Give thanks for everything you have and everything you are. If fear and doubt try to creep in, remind yourself who you are and who your God is.

Say this to yourself . . . I am amazing! I am strong! I am wisdom! I am a child of God! I was created with God's blueprint! I am love and I am loved! God's love and spirit are within me! I am and I have everything that I need. Remind yourself that you are fearfully and wonderfully made, like God tells us in the Bible.

Remember that God's love, wisdom, and timing are perfect. God doesn't always give us what we want, but He does give us what we need. Believe in yourself and nourish yourself. Be intentional with everything you do. By being intentional, we can be more aware of our present moment, and when we are present and aware, we can see everything with clarity. We can also nurture ourselves spiritually, emotionally, and physically.

Nurturing yourself means changing the food that you eat, the lifestyle you live, and the people you associate yourself with. It will make a big difference in your life and in your emotional and physical wellbeing when you choose health and positivity in your life.

As you go through challenges in life, you might feel tired and discouraged. It is okay to feel all these emotions—do not allow anyone to tell you otherwise.

Allow yourself to feel tired, angry, sad, weak, strong, joyful, everything you are feeling at that very moment. This emotional rollercoaster is part of your journey to find healing. Everyone processes their journey differently, and their timing might be different from yours. Remind yourself that you are not competing in a race to get to the finish line before others. No matter how long (or short) of a journey it is, the only important thing is for you to arrive at your destination.

Be proud of yourself. Be proud of your journey. Being a human being is not easy. Just breathe . . . and embrace all that you are. We all go through a rough time when we're healing from something. Let your courage push you to rise up through anything that stands in the way of your freedom.

As you walk along this path, you will gain more confidence and respect for yourself, and that, my friend, is pure strength. We come out of the ashes with God's love transformed and ready for the next phase in our lives. We come out stronger!

Never forget you are fearfully and wonderfully made! That is God's promise to you, and God never makes mistakes!

PART II
Healing Truths and the Human Body's Ability to Restore Itself

5

THE BODY'S ABILITY TO RESTORE ITSELF

The human body is so powerful and so incredible. We need to start believing that we have the ability to heal and regenerate our own cells. Whenever we are sick or injured, our bodies have a way to tell us. It also knows how to work on recovering and restoring itself. It may not be visible to us right away, especially when it's in the restorative state, but it does. It's like a miracle working behind the scenes.

For example, think of a scar on our skin. When we cut our skin, the blood cells in the body immediately start to form and create a clot to protect and stop the bleeding so our bodies don't lose blood. Over time, it starts to create a hard scab, and then you start seeing that the hard scab is no longer part of your skin. It falls off, and underneath it is brand new baby skin. This means the body has just regenerated many cells to restore itself. Our human bodies are beautiful miracles.

Billions of your cells regenerate every single day. Here are some other astounding statistics from Scientific American:[15]

- Tiny cells in your blood only live between three and 120 days.
- The cells that line your gut live less than a week.
- About 330 billion cells are regenerated daily.
- 30 trillion cells get replaced every 80 to 100 days.

I want you to know the truth about our bodies and their abilities to regenerate and heal themselves. I hope that by the little bit of information I share with you throughout my book, you'll have the knowledge and wisdom you need to take control of your life.

One of the most important things these facts tell me is that we have the power within us to heal ourselves. An incredible blueprint designed by God is working in perfect unison inside our bodies.

Breathing Exercises and Our Bodies

Breathing is extremely important for the overall functionally of our bodies. Without air, we die. This is something we all know, but we don't always think about it. We take breathing for granted. When we are mindful of how we breathe, we can do many things to physiologically change our bodies and minds. Breath is what gives life to all living things.

Before we go deep into this conversation, I want to share what I believe. When I think about it, I am in awe of how humans or all living things were formed and are living miracles. I believe in a God who created heaven and earth. No matter what everyone believes, we are all connected to our creator.

Genesis 2:7 says, "Then the LORD God formed man of the dust of the ground and breathed into his nostrils the breath of life, and man became a living being." I love this verse so much.

Every time I hear this verse, it reminds me of how important it is to breathe, because that is how we were formed. It's what gave us life, and it's what continues giving us life. I believe we should prioritize and pay more attention to our breathing. It's amazing how just a few simple minutes of breathing exercises immediately regulates our emotions and stabilizes our thoughts. Our bodies benefit tremendously from practicing breathing exercises.

Breathing exercises generate the oxygen that our bodies need daily. When we are mindful and we take deep breaths throughout the day, we are able to regulate our nervous systems and protect them from the daily stresses that come our way.

Stress is inevitable to avoid altogether, and that's why it's important to use tools like breathing exercises that are within reach for everyone to help combat stress. We need to believe that our bodies were created with many tools that are built-in to help us heal ourselves. They are within reach. If only we knew ourselves enough to know the power within us, we could live better and healthier lives. Unfortunately, with our current society and the way we live, we have been distracted and disconnected from our true selves.

How do we come back to ourselves the way we were originally made? How do we know if we can heal ourselves? How do we learn to tap into this potential? Here are a few things that I do that have been helping me heal from within.

- Prayer
- Meditation
- Exercise
- Walking in nature
- Eating healthy
- Journaling

When it comes to meditation, we cannot take the breath work out of meditation. Our brains work better when we take deep breaths. We think better and we feel better. Meditation is medicine.

Through meditation or breath work, our blood vessels can regenerate and allow our bodies to heal from the inside out. When you meditate and practice breath work, your body brings in new oxygen, and when we bring more oxygen into our blood vessels, our bodies function better.

How do we increase our blood oxygen levels in our bodies? Very simple—aerobic exercising is a great way to increase our oxygen levels. Meditation and breathing exercises, as I mentioned earlier. Quit smoking. Walk in nature. Practice yoga. Exercise. Keep yourself physically active. All of these methods will also help you nourish and create a strong immune system.

According to Dr. Joe Dispenza, "One of the core benefits of mindful meditation is that it forces a person to slow down and engage with the present moment. It does this by challenging them to pay more attention to the physical sensations of meditation, such as breathing, the feelings of energy within the body, and the sounds around them."[16]

When we are present, we become mindful, and that is how we allow ourselves to tap into our healing power. Dalai Lama XIV says, "There are only two days in the year that nothing can be done. One is called Yesterday and the other is called Tomorrow. Today is the right day to Love, Believe, Do, and mostly Live."[17]

Healing is not a simple thing, and it's not an easy thing to do. It will take practice, self- discipline, self-love, and, most importantly, consistency. Healing is a journey worth pursuing. Healing is a lifestyle. Live in the present. Live in the now.

A breathing method I personally do to help me with anxiety:

- 4 second inhale, 7 seconds of holding your breath, and 8 second exhale. If you are not familiar with meditation and breath work, you can reduce the amount of time. Start little by little and always remember that each healing journey is unique. Do what works for you and be kind to yourself.

The Power of Our Gut Microbiome

Our microbiomes are the ecosystems of all the microbes in our bodies: fungi, bacteria, and viruses. These microbes live in our bodies naturally, and some of them are good for us, while others can negatively affect our health.

Our microbiomes protect our health in many ways. They help our immune system and protect us from pathogens (bad disease-causing organisms). We want the good bacteria, not the bad bacteria. One of the main areas in our bodies that contain these microbes is our gut.

Our gut is not only responsible for digestion, but it has a direct link to our brain.

Ever heard someone ask, "What is your gut telling you?" or "Listen to your gut."? This type of intuition relates to a second brain in your body, hiding in your digestive system.[18]

So, if our gut bacteria is unhealthy, we will likely have issues with our brain, manifesting through depression, anxiety, irrational behaviors and other mental health challenges. These challenges can present in your life in the following ways:[19]

- Mood swings
- Sleepless nights
- Erratic behavior

When you suffer from these things, it causes problems in your family and work life. It essentially interferes in every aspect of your life.

Healthy gut bacteria, on the other hand, gives us the following benefits:[20]

- Reduces inflammation
- Engages our metabolism
- Fights unwanted viruses
- Eliminates bad bacteria
- Combats insulin sensitivity
- Controls our hormones

The healthier our gut microbiome is the more protection we will have for our immune system. Healthy bacteria act like an army against bad bacteria, which thrives when we eat toxic processed foods, or contaminated water, heavy metals, and pesticides. Even the air that we breathe can be toxic to our good microbes in our gut microbiome. Because sometimes it is hard to avoid all the things that can hurt our gut microbiome, it is important that we eat healthy and nourish our microbiome to keep it strong.

Your Immune System

Your immune system protects you from illness or anything that may want to attack. When we have strong and healthy immune systems, we don't get sick as often as others with compromised immune systems. Here are some examples of disorders that can weaken your immune system:[21]

- Severe combined immunodeficiency (SCID)
- Temporary acquired immunodeficiency (through viruses, medications, or cancer)
- Asthma
- Eczema
- Allergic rhinitis
- Type 1 diabetes

- Rheumatoid arthritis
- Lupus

If, however, you don't have any of these disorders, you can strengthen your immune system by eating naturally occurring probiotic and prebiotic foods, such as kimchi, sauerkraut, yogurt, kombucha, water kefir, tempe, garlic, onions, ginger, turmeric, fruits, and vegetables (These are only a few; there are many more I could list.).

Organic teas can also help strengthen your immune system. If you are willing, try drinking these teas instead of your morning coffee:

- Green tea
- Black tea
- Ginger
- Turmeric
- Chai tea

Chai is amazing—when you use the right ingredients. Make sure you pay attention to the amount of sugar you ingest with your chai tea. It can also be a disruptor to your gut because of the sugar content. Bad bacteria thrive on sugar.

Sleep is also very important for your immune system to grow strong and healthy. Try to reduce caffeine or eliminate it out of your system if you can. Caffeine will interfere with your ability to sleep restfully.

Stress is another disruptor to your immune system. Reducing your stress can have great benefits for your health system. I meditate almost daily; I can't imagine my life without meditation. It gives me wisdom, strength, internal peace, intuition, and awareness.

Awareness is powerful. When you become aware, you can change your life. You became who you are meant to be, and, all of a sudden, you start seeing your true potential. If you are not familiar with meditation, I would invite you to introduce meditation to your daily routine. It will change your life forever.

6
NUTRITION

Over the last forty years, we have been invaded by lies from the food industry and our health system. As a result of that, many Americans suffer from chronic disease and food-related illnesses such as diabetes, heart disease, cancer, etc.

The truth is that all these diseases are preventable or can be managed simply by changing our eating habits and lifestyles.[22] As of February 2020, the obesity rate in America increased to over 40 percent.[23] Believe it or not, over eleven million people around the world die every year from eating toxic and processed foods, and it's probably worse after the pandemic.[24] This is extremely sad and devastating news.

Please understand that, yes, sometimes traditional Western medicine will be necessary for certain illnesses, but if you respect your body and treat it holistically, it will get healthier. Then, more often than not, you won't need to take medication that, instead of healing your body long term, confuses your system, hindering your body's natural ability to heal itself.

Love your body, nourish it, and treat it with respect, and it will love you back.

We have an epidemic of pharmaceuticals in the food industry. The food is sprayed with pesticides and is genetically modified (GM) to the point of being dangerously toxic to our bodies.[25] Most GMO foods are altered to withstand various herbicides, then sprayed on entire fields of crops.[26] Nowadays, multiple herbicides are sprayed at once, including Roundup with the purpose to kill weeds but those weeds are already tolerant to Roundup.[27] And the toxic cycle continues. These toxic herbicides damage the soil microbiome, leading to a degradation of soils and plant health.[28] Pesticide and GMO technology are both part of a push for cheap food, but at what cost?

The fast-food industry is a perfect example of foods that rely on pesticides and GMOs that have no real nutrition and are leading us to an obesity epidemic in our country. Since obesity is a precursor to a whole host of health problems, including heart disease, high blood pressure, behavioral problems, and diabetes, these GMO foods can lead us to our deaths if we're not careful.

And adults aren't the only ones being victimized by the food industry. Our children are susceptible to this toxic industry as well. If it makes you angry to see the types of foods children get served every day in school, you are not alone—I am angry too!

Everything is loaded with sugar, artificial colors and flavors, processed meats, and GMO products. It's devastating for our younger generation; it's devastating for humanity in general. Yet even more devastating is how all this toxic food leads to another epidemic in our children—one of mental illness.

Our children are also being bombarded with violent video games. Based on my own observation, most children's behavior drastically changes after they play video games. This may not apply to all children, but my advice to all parents is to pay close attention to their children's behavior before and after they play video games. Some children are more sensitive than others. Their behavior goes from being happy and content to being moody and addicted, and they are not able to control their emotions. Some of them even become disrespectful and violent when their video games are cut off.

Video games stimulate their brain almost like cocaine to a person's behavior. Video games are extremely addictive and destructive to a child's emotional wellbeing. In my own opinion, I believe that the stimulation that the brain receives, along with the consumption of processed and sugary foods, has led our generation to suffer from increased amounts of diagnoses such as ADD, ADHD, depression, anxiety and all kinds of behavioral problems.

And then, to make things worse, the doctors within traditional Western medicine come in with a pill to "fix" the illness. This is completely unacceptable. We can do better than this.

The majority of these illnesses I'm talking about can be relieved and controlled with a healthier lifestyle, but not by only using traditional Western medication. Following a healthy lifestyle that is designed for your personal needs will make a big difference in your health. No pill will ever heal you fully. Western medicine may help with symptoms, but it will never heal you from the inside out, and you may end up with other health issues due to side effects. You need proper nutrition and being intentional with knowing what your body needs.

True health is not one size fits all. You need to truly know your body and know what hurts it and what helps it feels healthy. Do the work. Don't rely on pills to solve a problem that could be fixable by simply eating healthy and exercising. Take full responsibility for your health.

A perfect example is attention deficit disorder (ADD) and attention deficit hyperactive disorder (ADHD). Did you know that we can relieve the symptoms of ADD and ADHD with real nutrition, a healthy lifestyle, meditation, and exercise?[29]

Focus on adding the following foods into your diet if you're experiencing anxiety, depression, or a lack of focus or mental clarity:

- Blueberries
- Strawberries
- Leafy green vegetables
- Wild-caught salmon
- Sardines
- Nuts

We should be nourishing our brains with healthy organic brain foods. How do we want to live healthy lives if we don't feed and protect our brains? Our brains are what lead our bodies and actions daily. We can not be healthy if our brains are not healthy.

For our brains and bodies to be healthy, it is crucial to get rid of all synthetic sugars, artificial colors and flavors, processed foods, and alcohol in adults to heal the symptoms of ADHD.[30] Coffee can also be a negative stimulant for people with ADHD.[31]

Please understand, I am not saying to eliminate all the sugar. Make small changes. Eat an apple instead of a donut. Have water with lemon instead of a soda. Try making a meal at home instead of eating out. Start small so you don't overwhelm yourself.

Alcohol and coffee are very hard to eliminate, but you can start by reducing them a little bit at a time. Please listen to your body. If you have a sensitivity or an illness, make it a priority to eliminate anything that hurts your body. Check your behavior after you eat certain foods. Become aware of how your body feels after you eat or do something that makes your body feel either good or bad and make adjustments if necessary.

Don't reach for the easy and temporary fixes. It never works. Something you're eating might be giving you headaches or upset stomach, and you will be tempted to treat that symptom without questioning where the problem lies. Always remember that a pill will never fully heal you—it will only mask the root cause of your problem. The problem will still be there, and you will find yourself continually reaching for the pills that never quite give you the relief you need.

As an example, maybe drinking too much caffeine is giving you headaches. It's easy to reach for ibuprofen to hide the headache for a while, but if you keep drinking your caffeine, it's just going to come right back. This is also similar to how medical professionals treat your symptoms when you go to see them. Doctors and pharmacists are trained to treat the symptoms, but not to make the body healthy from the inside out, and the crazy cycle continues.

What is causing us to be sick? The food industry, the lifestyles we live, and the stress and anxiety we allow into our bodies. We are responsible for our health. No one else is.

Take responsibility and do your research. Educate yourself. Don't put your health into the hands of industries and people who don't have your best interests at heart.

Please also keep in mind that your environment will also contribute to your health or illness. For example, anxiety and depression can be created if you are in a toxic environment. Even if you try to be healthy or eat healthy, stress and toxic people can take a toll on your health.

Take a look at the crazy cycle of unhealthy eating habits, unhealthy behaviors, Western medicine, and the side effects of it all. One thing follows the other, and the unhealthy cycle repeats.

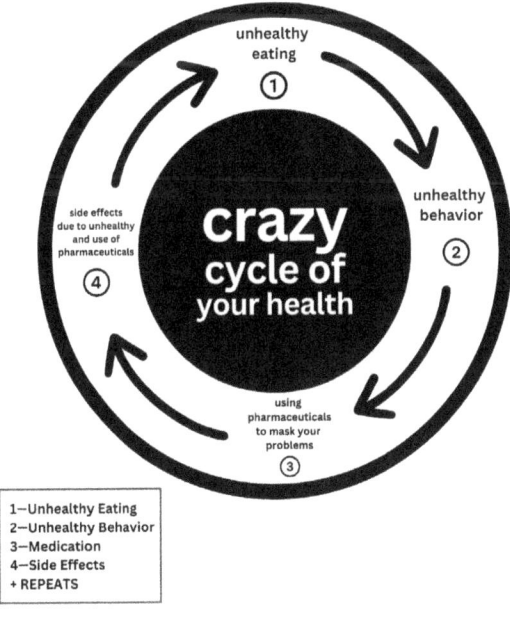

This is what most people do without even knowing they are following the unhealthy cycle:

1. Person A has an unhealthy lifestyle.
2. Person A eats processed foods.
3. Person A gets sick and goes to the doctor.
4. The doctor prescribes medication without diving deeper into the problem.
5. Person A continues unhealthy lifestyle, eating unhealthy foods, being inactive, etc.
6. Person A's symptoms return, and he/she goes back for more prescription medication.
7. Person A's gut is blocked and compromised from this unhealthy cycle.
8. Person A's liver is also overworking because of the prescription medication.

This cycle will not stop until you stop it.

Take care of your health. Your health is everything you have and the only thing that matters in this life.

7

MEDITATION

When we meditate, our brain cells are being regenerated and renewed, and in return, the effects of stress and anxiety or any illness changes as our brains' abilities to heal activates. Our brain is awakened to the ability to heal, sending signals to our body to heal our mental and physical traumas.

You can regulate your emotions through this process of meditation, which will put you in tune and harmony with your brain and body. Allowing this to happen will help you think clearer and make better decisions that lead you to a healthier state of being. This process is a huge step in our healing journey.

In 2014, a study at Johns Hopkins looked at the relationship between mindfulness meditation and its ability to reduce symptoms of anxiety, depression, and pain.[32]

Mindfulness meditation is an easy and free tool that anyone can access at any time, and it brings numerous health benefits.

According to one of my favorite doctors, Joe Dispenza D.C., meditation practices help rewire the brain. Dr. Joe Dispenza is a bestselling author of You Are the Placebo, Evolve Your Brain, Breaking the Habit of Being Yourself, and has received postgraduate training in neuroscience, brain functioning, memory formation, cellular biology, and neurology. In my own words, he's a genius.

Meditation opens up the doorway between the conscious and subconscious mind. Meditation is simply relaxing your body, such as when you are getting ready to fall asleep, but you are keeping your mind conscious while focusing on nothing. The process of getting your wandering mind back to focusing on nothing builds your ability to meditate and get the benefits of meditation.

Joe Dispenza says that in order to become somebody, we must become nobody in meditation. This means to let go of any thoughts, worries, and expectations in your mind during meditation to allow your brain to be in a restful state. When your brain is in a restful state and in the present moment, you access the power of meditation. You can become a new you.

Also, a study from Associated Chambers of Commerce and Industry of India (ASSOCHAM) says that twenty minutes of meditation is equivalent to 4-5 hours of deep sleep.[33] This study was part of their illness to wellness series themed "Emotional Wellness at Workplace."

The focus of the series was to create work/ life balance and better their emotional health while at work. How we breathe is prioritized when we are meditating.

There are different types of meditation for different needs. My favorite types of meditation are morning guided meditations, the 4-4-8 technique, and positive affirmation meditation.

The morning guided meditations that I like the most are by Sara Raymond, author of The Mindful Movement. There are several of her editions that I enjoy doing. One is a 15-minute meditation by Sara Raymond titled "Ignite Your Healing Power." Two other meditations from her that I love are "New Vision of You" and "Heal Your Body with Infinite Love and Gratitude."

The 4-4-8 breathing technique can help calm your nervous system when you are feeling stressed or anxious. This technique involves breathing in for a count of 4 seconds, holding the breath for 4 seconds, and then releasing it for a count of 8 seconds. I personally do this technique during the day when I feel stressed out, but you can do it anytime you feel that you need it.

I like to use the positive affirmation meditation technique in the morning when I am getting my kids ready for school. I like showing a positive example to my kids. Even though they pretend they are not listening, I know they are learning because I find them doing it sometimes when they think I am not watching. One of my favorite affirmations is the morning time "I AM" affirmations by Jason Stephenson. Another one that I really enjoy is the "You Are the Placebo" guided meditation by Dr. Joe Dispenza.

There are many amazing meditation techniques, and I hope that what I am sharing with you, is enough to get you started on your healing journey.

PART III
Healing Stories

Three Powerful Women

8

GRANDMA

Generational Curses and Generational Blessings

The following stories take a look deep inside the soul, the background of our ancestors, generational curses, and generational blessings. Everything you do in life, you will either bring a curse or a blessing to the generations that follow you; this is why understanding how important these concepts are can either make or break you on your journey to find healing.

Make sure you leave a beautiful and positive legacy to your next generations. It all starts with healing yourself. You set the example for future generations of your family through your words and actions. Your actions must match your words in order to be trustworthy.

How do we heal and become the best versions of ourselves? We achieve this through the work we do deep inside to heal our emotional traumas. When we do this, we give birth to new versions of ourselves that have the power to change the future as you shift your generational curses that were passed down to you by your ancestors.

I realized one day that even though we talk about generational curses, and we seem as though we are doing something to better ourselves and ultimately change our paths, somehow, we end up accepting the generational curses in our lives whether we like it or not. Why do we often fall into the same footsteps of our previous generations? Subconsciously, we accept what we were modeled from, at an early age. We fall into the same footsteps as our previous generations because we are familiar with them. It becomes such a habit that it almost feels like it's part of our DNA.

I believe generational curses are very real. Once we become aware of what they are and why we end up walking in the same footsteps as our past generations, we also become aware and empowered to break them.

This awareness is one of the first positive steps we can take toward healing ourselves. Not only that, but it helps you clear the way for the rest of your family and the other family members who haven't been born yet. We want the people we love to live their best lives, and that can start today with you.

We cannot forget that, along with our generational curses, we have generational blessings. Our generational blessings are what inspire us and make us proud of who we are and where we came from. One of my generational blessings comes from the story of my grandma and grandpa. I would like to share a few stories of some of my friends and some of my personal stories with the purpose of bringing awareness and hope to you.

Here is the story of my grandma and my grandpa as an example of generational curses, behavioral patterns, and generational blessings.

My grandma was a strong woman. She was a caring, independent, and well-respected businesswoman in her town with several businesses. One of them was a ranch where she raised beef cattle and horses, then she would sell them on the cattle market. She was meticulous and detail-oriented and took pride in everything she did; this was one of the things she was very proud of.

She also had a small Mexican bakery business. I can still smell the delicious aroma of homemade Mexican bread and pastries she made. Every time she made bread and pastries, she had all the family help with this business. She would assign a task to each of her grandkids and family members. Each of us would grab a piece of dough, and we would knead it by hand. Then we would cut it into small pieces to make a concha, bolillo, cupcake, or whatever we needed to make. It was a hard job, but very rewarding.

Once the bread and pastries were made, my grandma would fill a medium- to a small- sized bucket and sent all her grandkids to sell them to our neighbors. Once we sold all the bread and pastries, we would come home with all the money, and my grandma would give us a portion of it as a reward for our work.

What an amazing business mindset she had, and what a powerful lesson she taught to all her grandkids. A lot of who I am, I owe it to my grandma.

The most amazing thing I remember is that my grandma was always there by our sides, giving us an example and teaching us how to make the bread and pastries. She would bake them in a wood-fired brick oven. The smell was unforgettable.

She also had a cannabis side business, believe it or not. As a child, I didn't like what she was doing and at times, I felt embarrassed because of the reputation that the cannabis business has had for many years, but now that I can understand everything she did and why she did it, I think to myself, Wow, what an amazing and incredibly intelligent woman she was. My grandma was a woman full of wisdom and knowledge, and I have no words to express how honored and proud I am to be her granddaughter.

The work that she did with the cannabis business was impressive. She cultivated everything from the seed to the time the plant needed to be processed and packed. She needed it for medicinal reasons. She had arthritis and I remember how she would mix cannabis with alcohol and would store it in a jar for a few days and then she would rub it on her knees or any muscle that had pain. She was extremely intelligent and savvy. The people she did business with respected and trusted her.

She did a lot to bring financial freedom to our family with all the businesses she had.

My grandma always had a story of wisdom to share with our family and she was also very funny with her words. Sometimes she would make a comment with words we never heard of before, and we would ask what she meant with that or if she made up those words. Every single word was found in the dictionary. It was impressive.

My grandma was an orphan child; her mother died when she was only eight years old. When my great-grandma gave birth to my grandma's baby sister, she ended up having health complications and died unexpectedly. After a couple of years, my great grand father remarried. At that time, my grandmother was about ten years old. Her stepmother was mean and calculated. She would lie to get the kids in trouble and hide the food from them to punish them.

At the age of fifteen, my grandma stood against her stepmother. She ended up having to fight her physically to defend her baby sister. This is very sad because these types of stories happen more often than we would like to hear.

One day, my grandma's stepmother was hitting her baby sister. My grandma couldn't take it anymore, so she lashed at her stepmother and defended her baby sister.

My grandma was a person not to be messed with. Once she had it, she had it, and she wasn't going to take it. She was a woman who carried herself with dignity, justice, and respect everywhere she went. And she was also a woman of wisdom, honor, and determination. She had these traits back then, and she used them to take action to defend her baby sister. From then on, her stepmother never attempted to hurt or disrespect my grandma nor her baby sister ever again.

My grandma is one of my heroes in life. A lot of who I am, I am because of her example. Her legacy will live for a very long time. She was a woman of strength who endured a lot of pain and suffering. Any healing she did, she had to learn on her own.

She was excellent at everything she did. She knew how to do work normally thought of as a man's work. She knew how to be a farmer and grow her own food. She knew how to build homes from scratch and how to raise livestock.

She knew how to make her own clothes from scratch. She knew how to bake and cook, and she knew how to be a businesswoman. She was an excellent negotiator and an excellent communicator. Did I tell you how she learned to read? Through reading the Bible and the newspaper. How amazing is that? She was an amazing leader.

My grandma could do practically everything she set her mind to, but there was one thing she didn't get a chance to learn or master. This one thing is crucial in life, and guess what this one thing is? She never learned how to heal her emotional trauma.

Unfortunately, my grandma carried a ton of responsibilities. She had to suppress a lot of pain during her life because that was what society taught her. That is what society has been teaching us for many generations. We need to start making changes as we talk about it, and as we learn to heal.

My grandma had to be strong because she didn't have a choice. She was a survivor. Unfortunately, many of the responsibilities she had, didn't even belong to her. She just didn't know how to let go of them. Others were more important to her, and she would look out for everyone in our family.

She was always the one who would clean up every mess my grandpa or anyone in the family would make. My grandma would always come to the rescue to pay my grandpa's (or anyone else's) financial debt whenever it became a big problem.

Grandpa's Gambling

My grandpa was a sweet, funny guy and a very laid-back person. He had a comfortable job he loved; he worked as a commercial bus driver. My grandpa didn't put much effort into working harder because my grandma would always provide for the family. Every day, one would see him driving from town to town, singing, making jokes, and making people laugh as he transported passengers from town to town.

As a child, I didn't see the deep problem in their relationship. You see, the problem was that because my grandpa was too laid back, my grandma had to take on responsibilities that technically belonged to my grandpa. As a result of that, my grandma was frustrated, disappointed, and resentful toward my grandpa.

She was emotionally and physically exhausted. My grandpa didn't show that he was aware of her disappointment. He didn't make an effort to change his behavior, which caused more stress for grandma and their relationship.

My grandpa had a gambling problem, gambling with his buddies almost daily. One day, he went as far as to gamble away the title of their home. My grandma had to come up with the money he lost in order to recover the title.

Can you imagine this? This is deep, painful, and very disappointing to have to deal with—a partner who tears your finances apart instead of being protective and working together to build more. This behavior is a form of betrayal that feels like a punch in the gut, and it is hard to recover from because you really have nothing if you can't trust the partner you picked to live with for the rest of your life.

My grandma took on such a heavy burden that it was not physically or emotionally healthy for her. She lived her life with constant stress. It was hard for me to see her once I got old enough and could understand the amount of stress she carried. She didn't know how to relax.

From my perspective, it seemed hard for my grandma to relax because she didn't have anyone to support her emotionally. The partner she picked was not reliable. Their relationship was not balanced, and when a relationship is not balanced, it becomes dysfunctional.

I hope that when men read this book, they can see deep inside of them and ask themselves if what they are doing is supportive of their wives or partners who are strong and independent.

I often see this problem—where men get comfortable when they are married to women who are strong and independent. Somehow, they stop trying their best or stop working, and they think that the relationship is going to be healthy.

Maybe that is the case in some couples, but not in most couples. That is not the story I hear from most of my friends and women I talk to. This is one of the reasons many women decide to leave their partners and live on their own, focusing on themselves and their children instead of having to deal with a lazy, passive, and irresponsible partner.

Here is what many women have told me on this topic:

- I don't need another child to take care of.
- I want to be taken care of and feel like I have a partner who supports me emotionally.
- I want a partner who is driven and wise with his finances.
- I don't want to feel like I have to be the one making all the family decisions by myself.

- I want a partner who is present emotionally.
- I want a partner who is in tune with our goals and dreams as a couple and as a family.
- I want a partner who is not afraid to lead.

You see, even though strong women may not need to be taken care of financially, they may still want to feel like they are not alone in taking on responsibilities. When strong women are financially independent, they also want their partners to be strong emotionally and financially. They don't want their partners to stop pursuing their dreams, and they don't want their partners to sit back and wait for the women to take action on everything.

When men don't take responsibility for their role as men and leaders, the relationship deteriorates over time. This is the truth, whether we like to hear it or not. As much as we like to paint things pretty, the relationship will eventually turn stale because most women become emotionally drained and let down by their partners.

Men are meant to be the givers and providers, and women are designed to be the receivers. God created us this way for a reason. We can't change God's original masculine and feminine design. Society has a different agenda, and it has created a toxic and very dysfunctional outcome in the role of men and women and each individual's responsibilities.

This has to change if we want to preserve the true and original roles of male and female. The connection between male and female is sacred, and its beautiful when true femininity and true masculinity come together. Let's keep it this way!

Emotional Pain Has Physical Consequences

My grandma was a very strong woman, and she carried her life with dignity and respect. She conquered many obstacles in her life, but she carried a lot of hurt and resentment inside of her.

This resentment caused her to live a life with constant stress, not knowing the stress was going to eventually kill her one day.

It is crucial that we all think of this and start working on our healing journeys. Work through your emotional traumas and start your healing journey for the sake of your physical and emotional health.

My grandma, unfortunately passed away a few years ago. She was diagnosed with cancer in her stomach in 2012, battling with it on and off for years. After a couple years, she seemed to be doing good, and she thought the cancer was gone forever.

At the beginning of 2017, she felt ill again. Her doctors told her she still had cancer, and it was spreading to the rest of her organs. They were not sure they could do anything to save her. She tried different remedies and medicine in hopes that she would recover, but she could never completely recover.

Unfortunately, she passed away August 22nd of 2017 at seventy-four years old. I never thought she would leave so soon. We did remedies, chemo, and many other things. We also sent our prayers up to God, but nothing worked. I felt devastated. She was the glue of the family.

Every time I needed advice for anything in my life, I would go to her. It was hard to want to call her and not be able to do it. This is one thing in life that we will never get used to, nor will understand. When we miss our deceased loved ones and we can't just grab the phone and call them. All we can do is close our eyes and talk to them. Even if we can't hear them or feel them physically, I know they can hear us. Just close your eyes and tell them how you feel. We will see them again once we are all reunited in heaven.

When my grandma passed away, I had so many questions. What if she knew how to heal her emotional trauma and learned to let go of responsibilities that didn't belong to her? Maybe if she knew, she would have lived a longer and healthier life. Nobody told her or mentioned anything about the importance of healing her childhood traumas. Not even the doctors mentioned anything about it when she first was diagnosed.

I didn't even know anything about the importance of working on our emotional traumas in order to heal our physical diagnosis until just a few years ago. When grandma was sick, I didn't know the importance of letting go of anything that hurt us emotionally and physically for the sake of our health. Please understand that this process is not easy, but it is possible and the rewards are priceless.

If I knew then what I know now, I would've taken her to a healing center where people focus on working through their emotional traumas and their healing journeys. There are many of them, and unfortunately, not very many people talk about them.

Dr. Joe Dispenza is a great example of a medical professional who understands how important this healing is for our longevity. He has many amazing stories of people who have healed themselves from cancer and many other diagnoses.

I wish I would have known about him before my grandma was diagnosed with cancer. If I had learned about him sooner, I would have helped my grandma work through her childhood traumas and heal her emotions so she could have lived a longer life.

Bruce Lipton once said, "The moment you change your perception is the moment you rewrite the chemistry of your body."[34] This reminds me of a Bible verse that says:

> "'Then you will know the truth, and the truth will set you free'" (John 8:32).

The Bible also says in Romans 12:2, "Do not conform to the pattern of this world, but be transformed by the renewing of your minds. Then you will be able to test and approve what God's will is—his good, pleasing and perfect will." This is very important because it teaches us that when we renew our minds, we renew our lives.

Dr. Joe Dispenza also says, "If our thoughts can make us sick, is it possible that the same thoughts can make us well? The answer is absolutely yes!"[35] Donny Miller says, "In an age of information, ignorance is a choice."[36] There is so much wisdom in these words.

I want you to see that we have the power to change our thoughts, and when we become AWARE of our thoughts and our toxic behaviors, we can make positive changes in our minds, bodies, and lives.

I strongly believe in the words of wisdom that are in the Bible. They give hope and life to us. God knew we were going to need them in our lives as we experience hardship.

If we want to rewire and renew our minds, we must become AWARE. AWARENESS creates HEALING, and through ACTION, we create TRANSFORMATION. When we become aware, we can transform ourselves into new and healthy human beings. The answer is not outside of you—the answer is within you. You simply need to become AWARE of the power within you to start your healing journey.

In 2020, I had a revelation while I was fasting and meditating for direction in my personal life. I felt like the voice of my grandma, grandpa, and my beloved uncle, who had also passed away, were talking to me and whispering in my ear.

They revealed things to me I could not fully understand at first, but after a good amount of time meditating and praying, I could understand their message. Their presence and spirit felt so real within my spirit that it's hard to explain everything in detail with words.

In my mind, I was re-living their lives, and they told me I had to heal my traumas to heal my past, present, and future generations. They told me I had to let go of any emotional pain I was holding inside, and I needed to work on releasing any responsibilities that didn't belong to me.

They showed me the image of myself where I was following the same footsteps as my grandma, who took on responsibilities that didn't belong to her, responsibilities that made her live with disappointments and stress, that ultimately ended up killing her. Somehow, she felt responsible for everyone in her life.

After they showed me what I was doing, I understood what I had to do to live a healthy life and start making changes in my life from then on. I had to start working on healing my childhood traumas and disappointments, and I had to start working on healing my generational curses.

I had to let go of responsibilities that didn't belong to me. I had to walk away from things that didn't serve me, and I had to let go of the people who took energy from me in negative ways. On top of that, I had to learn to build healthy boundaries for the sake of my emotional and physical health.

Walk away from people who keep you in constant stress. Your gut feeling will always tell you who those people are. Listen to your gut and start healing your emotional traumas so your present and future generations can reap the fruits of your healing.

My healing journey is still a work in progress, but thanks to my grandma, my grandpa, and my uncle who revealed such amazing truths to me, I can heal and I can show my children the importance of healing our emotional traumas and the importance of regulating our emotions for the sake of our health.

My life is different now. I am teaching my children the importance of meditation and prayer and how to become aware of their spiritual intuition that reveals hidden truths. I am teaching them the importance of self- regulating their emotions. I am teaching them as I practice it myself.

As we become spiritually aware, we can take action to walk on the path toward our healing journey, a path also filled with wisdom and emotional maturity.

From now on, my priority is to show my children and my readers the importance of healing their traumas, letting go of responsibilities that do not belong to them, and loving and nurturing their bodies, minds, and souls. Knowing how to self-regulate your emotions is wisdom at its best.

9

ANA

A Traumatic Childhood

Ana is a caring woman, a woman of faith, and a giver. However, she often gave too much because she didn't know how to say no. She always looked for the good in people because she cared and loved them, but when it came to her, she was hard on herself.

One big reason why some people tend to be hard on themselves is because they might've had a parent who was hard to please or emotionally manipulative or emotionally immature. Throughout their younger years, they probably tried very hard to get their parents' approval, yet that approval was hard won—or not received at all. This type of upbringing instills the idea in them that they are never quite good enough, and it can often cause them to question everything they do.

Ana was a people pleaser, which is not a good thing when you are trying to heal and have to say no to things and people who take advantage of you. They also might try to control you through manipulation and gaslighting.

Ana had difficult trials she went through in life, as we all do, but she would always find a way to rise up and tune into her intuition to learn and become a better person. She had to empower herself to turn her mess into a message. Her passion was always to help and to make things better for others. She had compassion and cared for people probably a bit too much.

As Ana gave more and more of herself to the people around her, little by little, she forgot to recharge herself and protect her emotional energy. She would help to the point of putting her needs aside because she felt guilty if she didn't help. This guilt often told her lies about herself; for instance, she thought it made her a selfish person if she didn't please others.

Unfortunately, she carried trauma from her childhood. Growing up, her mom would gaslight her and would often make manipulative comments. Her mother was not aware of her behavior because she didn't have a mature view of parenting. She didn't know how to talk to her kids or how to love and respect them.

Ana was a very intuitive person from an early age. However, according to her mom, Ana was not a good daughter because she would speak up, and she would disagree with the way her mom would talk to her. Despite the way her mother made her feel, though, Ana would still comply to keep the peace.

At the age of nine, Ana's beloved stepfather was tragically killed. To this day, she doesn't know if his death was an accident or maybe someone planned to kill him deliberately. His death changed Ana's life forever. She was in shock when she received the news. She was excited to celebrate her ninth birthday, and she had to go from feeling excited to receiving the shocking news of her father's death.

Her stepfather believed in God and loved Ana's mother dearly. He took care of Ana and her siblings as if they were his own. This amazing man loved his family, and he was always ready to help others. He loved his friends, and one of his favorite hobbies was to play basketball.

Every evening, he'd play basketball with his friends. One day, he was invited by one of his friends to have a few beers and hang out right after the basketball game. After a while, one of the guys started an argument with another guy. After a heated moment of arguing, one of them pulled out a gun.

They continued arguing, and then Ana's stepfather tried to get in between to stop the argument, but the gun went off. One bullet took Ana's dad away forever.

In situations like this, our immediate reaction is, how can life be so cruel? How do we bear with this amount of pain as human beings? How do we mourn the death of our loved ones, especially when our loved ones are taken away by accident? All these questions have no answer.

We just keep going as we try our best to heal our wounds and get better, not bitter. Ana tried her best to see the best in everything and in everyone.

She grew up fast after that tragic event and missed her stepfather every day. She could not express her feelings due to the shocking and painful news. After her stepfather was buried, she started crying, but because she had so much emotional and physical pain, she couldn't even cry because she found it difficult to even breathe. It's hard to explain the pain she was going through. Her chest was tight, and she felt deep, excruciating pain.

She didn't understand why that was happening to her. Her mother was devastated and in extreme pain as well. Her mother was about eight months pregnant at that time. Can you imagine the unbearable pain her mother went through?

As Ana felt alone and confused about life and the tragic death of her stepfather, she made a prayer to God at the age of nine during one of her intense crying spells. She asked God to be her father: "Father God, please be my dad. I need you to watch over me and guide me as I go through life. Please be with me." She wasn't sure if God was truly there or if God was even real, but she trusted him.

Ana went on with her life. It was not easy as years went by, but she always had strong faith and intuition to help her maneuver through life. She had love and compassion for helping people.

When we go through devastating moments, we become the caretakers, the ones who always want to help others so they don't have to go through the pain we experienced. Ana became a caretaker with almost anyone she knew.

Psychologically speaking, could it be possible that Ana never healed from the pain she had to go through when her stepfather was killed? She was compensating for her pain. Deep in her subconscious mind, she felt the need to help others because, deep in her heart, she thought she could minimize her pain by being of service to others. She also didn't want others to go through the pain she experienced. Little by little, she started carrying stress and responsibilities that didn't belong to her.

As Ana continued living with her mother and having a hard time with her being emotionally harsh and manipulative at times, it became hard for Ana to continue living with her. Ana's grandma lived close by, so she decided to move in with her.

Ana was not a rebellious child, all she wanted was her mother to treat her with respect and acceptance. Ana's mom showed favoritism between her own children. It was very hard and sad for Ana to see that behavior coming from her own mother. Ana didn't want to be in a toxic relationship with her mother, so she thought it was best to detach from her. The constant manipulation and harsh comments made Ana detach from her mother emotionally and physically as soon as she was able to.

It appears as though her mother held some resentment towards her, or maybe it had nothing to do with her; maybe it was her mother's insecurities and ignorance as she tried to be a mother with no proper guidance. Unfortunately, some people hurt others, including their loved ones, when they don't know how to regulate their emotions.

Ana has nothing but love and compassion for her mother because she sees her mother as a person who was in survival mode and did things out of ignorance. Because her mother lacked the knowledge and maturity she needed to be a good mother, Ana doesn't blame her mother for anything. Ana believes that when parents raise their children with manipulation or immaturity, they simply lack knowledge and love for themselves and others.

The environment Ana grew up in made her feel unheard and disrespected. Her family often made fun of her and joked about her, and if she cried or didn't like what they said, she simply needed to toughen up, because according to them, "it was just a joke." Gaslighters often say this to put the responsibility on someone else for the things they say or do. When somebody says this, they are essentially saying, "You are the one with the problem if you can't take the joke. That's not my fault." This type of environment is emotionally harmful, toxic, and not acceptable whatsoever.

Growing up this way created deep emotional wounds in Ana. As she got older, she created walls of protection around herself and emotionally detached herself from her mother and anybody who would hurt or disrespected her.

The people who believed in her and saw her potential were her uncle, whom she called her dad, and her grandmother. Her uncle was a great father figure to her. He took care of Ana, and he would defend her when she got verbally mistreated by her mom or her siblings.

Though often misattributed to Maya Angelou, Carl W. Buehner once said, "I've learned that people will forget what you said, people will forget what you did, but people will never forget how you made them feel."[37]

It is crucial that we speak and treat our children with kindness and respect. We should allow them to form their unique personality. Guide them in the right direction, but always respect and honor them for who they are. It is crucial to be kind and gentle to their spirits.

When we try to compare our children's personalities and treat them badly because they are not the way we "want them to be," we create emotional damage and separation. This behavior is toxic and disrespectful. Every child is different, and we need to love them according to their own love language. We need to look deep into their souls and make them feel loved, respected, and safe.

According to Gary Chapman in The 5 Love Languages, everyone interprets love in different ways. Here are the five ways Chapman outlined in his book:[38]

- Words of Affirmation
- Quality Time
- Receiving Gifts
- Acts of Service
- Physical Touch

We need to nurture our children with love, respect, and compassion. Allowing them to grow into their individuality is critical, and most importantly, we need to teach our children that this is healthy by showing them examples through our own lives. The example we model for our children and how we treat them will either cause them to shut down emotionally or it will help their personality to bloom, allowing them to become confident, secure, and compassionate adults.

Please know that no matter what way you were treated as a child and no matter what kind of childhood trauma you may be carrying, you can heal and you can become the best version of yourself. Start by loving and nurturing yourself as you learn how to let go of anything that holds you back emotionally.

There is always somebody who makes a positive impact in your life. As you try to heal, hold on to that and encourage yourself. It is amazing to see the miracles that can happen when we build a positive word and when we are kind and gentle with ourselves and others. It brings healing to our spirit and ultimately to our minds and bodies. Love and the power of positive words can heal anything!

Thankfully, Ana learned from her grandma and her uncle, who was also her stepfather. Yes, you heard it right. Ana's mom and her second cousin were together. Not my cup of tea, but discussing this subject is not my priority here, so let's leave it for another time.

Ana's stepdad and her grandma made a great impact on her life, and believe it or not, Ana also learned from her mother. She learned what not to do. This experience from her childhood helped her learn how not to talk to her children and how not to make them feel.

She learned to look deep into herself and her flaws, not in a judgmental way but in a way that she could build a better future for herself. Ana was determined to be a better mother, daughter, sister, and friend. She wanted to break down the chains of emotional pain and trauma. She wanted to break down the chains of generational curses.

Her mother was not a bad person; she just didn't know how to raise a child in a healthy way, emotionally speaking. Ana's mother had a naïve way of thinking, maybe because she was sheltered by her parents. She didn't know how to be responsible or emotionally mature.

Ana's grandma was Ana's role model. Ana looked up to her with admiration and respect. She was a strong woman who had a strong work ethic and went above and beyond with everything she did. On the other hand, Ana's mother had everything and didn't have to work hard to provide for herself. She was naïve about life and about responsibilities.

You see, Ana's mom grew up thinking that she needed to depend on a man or others for her needs while she was hurting herself and others. With that mindset she became a victim and toxic as well. She expected everyone around her to provide everything she needed. She didn't know how to provide for herself nor she wanted to.

Her mindset was that she didn't have to work on herself to better herself or sharpen her skills for a career. Ana didn't fully understand how this could happen when her grandma was an amazing example of a strong woman who worked hard to provide and better herself.

Ana's mom didn't allow herself to mature because she got married in her teens. Unfortunately her first marriage didn't survive. She would go from making one mistake to making another mistake without being able to mature.

When she attempted to be in a relationship for the second time, she met Ana's dad. He sounded like a good man but he was not. From the stories Ana heard, he provided for her mother above and beyond, but he was abusive and cheated on her multiple times.

The life of Ana's mom was difficult and nothing was going to change unless she changed her mindset. Her way of thinking was not healthy for herself because this type of thinking can cause people to become victims and also manipulate others without even being aware of it.

Because they are always provided for, they can become self-centered, manipulative, and even abused by the partners they choose. They often go on in life making mistake after mistake instead of fixing themselves to eliminate their toxic patterns.

In order for us to change our outcomes, we need to examine ourselves and be truly honest with ourselves. We need to allow ourselves to mature as we heal our emotional traumas.

Look deep inside yourself and ask yourself these questions:

- Who am I?
- Who made me this way?
- Was it the lies of society?
- Was it my childhood trauma?
- Do I like who I am, or do I need to work on healing my trauma?

- Do I like how I treat myself and others?
- Who do I want to be?

Often, we fall into the lies of society and the negative words instilled in our minds from an early age. Here are a few lies I want you to eliminate from your thinking:

- You are a selfish person if you choose yourself.
- You are stupid.
- You are bad if you choose to walk away from family members who hurt you.
- Your health is determined by your genes.
- Generational curses are destined and cannot be broken.
- You are not enough.
- You need to follow the rules to keep the peace.
- You must keep quiet because you do not want to disappoint anyone.

Isn't it funny how all these lies may seem innocent, but they can be detrimental to our lives and to our healthy future selves? Most of us live our lives trying to please people because we were raised with the idea that this is how we are supposed to be.

We were taught from a very early age to keep quiet because we don't want to disrupt the "peace." We keep quiet as we see so much cruelty and heartless behavior from others.

We must expose evil, confusion and dishonest people or situations by speaking up and becoming the game changers, the peacemakers. In other words, you should be an advocate for peace and transparency, even if you have to create a war against injustice, confusion and evil in order to bring true peace.

When we speak the truth, we will start a war against confusion, injustice, and evil, but eventually, we will bring peace and true healing to ourselves and others. **Be a warrior for peace.**

Most of us live our lives wanting to please people because we were taught from an early age that this is what good boys and good girls do. We don't want to disappoint anyone if we say no. This is detrimental to ourselves and our inner peace. It confuses you. It eats you from the inside out and destroys your confidence, true power, and full potential.

If we become mindful and live with awareness of who we are and what we choose, we can break our generational curses. As we operate in a mindful state, we can become the best version of ourselves. You will see that you no longer live or behave the same way our parents or grandparents did.

Our human nature has the tendency to lean towards the bad habits and behaviors we saw growing up. If we grew up seeing toxic relationships, we usually end up in toxic relationships without even knowing it.

A perfect example of generational curses is Ana's experience with her relationship. Ana ended up in a similar relationship as she had with her mom as a child. Ana's mom was emotionally manipulative, and she had a tendency to play the victim to avoid responsibility for her actions. She would blame and gaslight as she played the victim when she felt threatened or confronted.

Her mom would use manipulation and favoritism to get her kids to obey her or do things for her. Ana hated this behavior because she wanted justice every time she felt like her mom was being unfair or manipulative. Ana was confused and felt hurt and resentful towards her mom. Ana didn't understand why her own mother would treat her the way she treated her.

A mother should never talk to her children with hurtful and manipulative words. This is emotional abuse and very damaging to a child. She wanted to please her mother, as most children try to do, but she was not happy with pleasing toxic behaviors. When the person who manipulates you is your own mother, this is a hard pill to swallow, and it is very hard to heal these types of wounds.

Ana left the home at the age of fifteen. She wanted to be independent and walk away from the toxic relationship she had with her mom. She didn't want to be near her mom's toxic behavior.

The example that Ana saw coming from her mom was embarrassing to Ana. Ana's mom went from toxic relationship to toxic relationship, and she didn't seem to take charge of her life. She always depended emotionally and financially on her mom, her romantic partners, or her children.

There would always be an excuse every time she had to take responsibility for herself. She would get angry and play the victim if she was confronted, so Ana couldn't really tell her how she felt. Ana tried doing that a couple of times, but things would always turn against Ana.

When Ana moved away from her mom, she still had a consistent relationship with her. After all, you can't really fully cut ties with your parents. Your parents will always be your parents, no matter how toxic they may be.

Ana lived her life and made herself independent, and she tried everything in her power to have a different life from that of her childhood experience. Or at least she thought so.

When Ana started dating, she didn't know why she would end up in relationships with men who were manipulative, emotionally immature, and had victim-like behaviors. She would end up with two types of men. Men who were extreme Alpha—the toxic kind of Alpha— and the weak men who would play the victim and would gaslight her and manipulate her.

She would walk away immediately from the toxic Alpha men because they reminded her of her biological father, and she didn't want to have anything to do with that.

She would fall for the soft and weak men because she felt the need to help them, but the more she did for them, the more she felt emotionally drained and confused.

Ana felt as though she had to please and almost save every man she dated. The majority of men she dated were immature, insecure, and emotionally broken. Somehow, she felt responsible for them. Ana found it hard to let go of those unhealthy relationships. She didn't know why she would end up in those types of relationships.

It didn't occur to Ana that the reason why she would find herself in emotionally unstable relationships had to do with her childhood trauma. It had to do with her experience with her mother, who would play the victim when it was convenient to her.

Ana was an empath who had no idea that she needed to recognize her childhood traumas and start healing them in order for her to have a different and healthy outcome in her life.

When an empath gets in a relationship with a person who plays the victim in order to avoid responsibility, it is very hard to break out of that cycle because the empath will naturally feel the need to nurture and help the person playing the victim, even if it drains them emotionally and physically.

Unfortunately, the empath doesn't get out of the relationship because they feel responsible for the other person's physical and emotional wellbeing. The other person, on the other hand, doesn't let go because they are in their comfort zone. This cycle is toxic and very hard to break out of. It takes guts to do it. You need to become aware of the toxic patterns to start making healthy changes. Both people can definitely become healthy, but they both need to work on their traumas in order to become healthy.

When Ana started working on her childhood traumas and focused on her emotional healing, she realized that she had to use her voice to say no in order for her life to start changing.

She didn't know that her coping mechanism was to come to the rescue to try to save and please others because she lived her life trying to please her mother. Ana wanted her mother to accept her, and she thought that pleasing or enabling and rescuing others was the answer. This way of living is never healthy nor sustainable. It's exhausting and emotionally draining.

Ana decided to be what our society may call, "selfish" to protect her health and her emotional energy. It became important for her to pour into her spirit and soul before giving to others.

She realized that she had to put herself first, and she had to protect her emotional energy. She had to say no to negative people or anyone who depleted her energy, rather than uplifted her energy.

She also learned to let go of negative people and any negative environment she found herself in. It was also important for her to let go of any responsibilities that didn't belong to her. She learned to put the oxygen mask on herself before attempting to help others. Ana felt she would lose her true purpose in life if she didn't grow stronger and more disciplined in her responses to others.

You see, when we give and give, we become dry and drained. We suffer and we don't understand why. It disconnects us from our intuition and true calling. We become confused and emotionally depleted.

We need to do our self-check, emotionally speaking, every day, believe it or not, in order to keep this confusion at bay. If we do this, when life's challenges come our way, we can recognize them, fight back against them, and get up stronger.

At the age of eighteen, Ana became a Christian. She learned to pray for everyone, including her future husband. She thought she was doing everything "right".

She prayed for her future husband. She prayed for her family, her friends, and herself. Ana became actively involved in her church community.

She was a part of a Christian band who ministered to the youth. She also held a youth Bible study. When she attended Bible college, she also went a few times to minister to the people in jail with a group of missionaries. She loved her life during this phase.

Everything sounded great and promising for Ana, but what do we do when bad things happen to people—or I should say—what do we do when bad things happen to good people?

When she got married, she thought everything was going to be amazing because she prayed for her husband, and when you pray, everything goes well, right? Well, not necessarily. That is immature, spiritually speaking.

Let's go back to when she became a Christian, and she learned to pray for her husband. Unfortunately, we are a bit naïve after we give our lives to God. We forget we are humans, and no matter what we believe, we are still going to go through challenges in life.

The question is not "if" bad things are going to happen but rather "if" and "when" bad things happen, how do we come out of the ashes still loving and trusting God and ourselves? There will always be challenges we will face in life. Our mindsets will determine our outcomes as we go through challenges.

We need to allow challenges to run their course, and we need to continue trusting our creator, because only He sees our future. There is always a light at the end of the tunnel, and there is always a way to turn our mess into a message.

I believe our purpose in life arrives when we come out of the ashes with a bright light radiating from within us, and with empathy for others, uplifting others with our actions and our testimony. Our testimony has more power than anything we say or do. Your testimony has power, don't keep it to yourself.

John 16:33 says, "'I have told you these things, so that in me you may have peace. In this world you will have trouble. But take heart! I have overcome the world.'"

It is hard to hear that we will "have tribulations," because we all know how cruel life can be at times. Life is messy and painful and confusing, but we cannot forget that it is also beautiful and worth living, no matter what. We cannot allow the bad things that happen to us to turn us bitter and with no purpose.

I love this quote by Josh Shipp, an author and motivational speaker: "You either get bitter or you get better. You either take what has been dealt to you and allow it to make you a better person or you allow it to tear you down. The choice does not belong to fate, it belongs to you."[39]

He could not have said it any more perfect than this. Based on my perspective and my struggles in life, I strongly believe that the challenges that come our way are there to either teach us and to give us the choice to become stronger and wiser or to become victims. The choice is up to us.

Ana prayed for her husband before she even knew who her husband was going to be. Unfortunately for Ana, things didn't go as beautiful as she thought.

Ana thought that once you became a Christian, and especially when you pray or prayed for your husband or anything, and when you are doing everything right, God will bless you. Again, not necessarily.

Ana was a bit naïve and in love when she made the decision to marry her husband. When it comes to a healthy relationship, love is not enough. There are many more things that are necessary for a marriage to be successful.

All our choices bring consequences. Some are positive and some are negative. We all need to understand that it is crucial to fully know the person we want to create a future with.

Discovering their ins and outs is critical. We need to know who they are when they are sad or angry. We need to know how they handle themselves when they face challenges and how they are going to treat you regardless of how they feel.

We need to know what their dreams and goals are, physically, financially, and emotionally speaking. Are they going to protect you, or are they going to throw you under the bus when it feels beneficial to them?

Are they going to help you feel safe and secure, or are they going to make you feel anxious and stressed out? Are they going to truly love you, or are they going to manipulate or gaslight you when things don't go their way?

Are there any health problems or emotional traumas in that person you should be aware of? Are there any addictions or toxic behaviors that might affect the way the person thinks or makes decisions in life? Are they healthy when it comes to handling money? Is their relationship with food healthy? Believe me, you are going to need to ask yourself all these questions if you want to land a healthy relationship.

All these issues will affect your life and the ability to create your future together. It is crucial to know these things, because they will affect your relationship big time.

How is their relationship with their mother and father? What is their family's health history? What triggers them in challenging situations, and how do they handle difficult situations? Are they able to regulate their emotions?

What is their definition of love? What kind of love did they grow up in? Did they even have love and affection from their mother and father growing up? Were they in a caring environment growing up, or did they grow up in a harsh and abusive environment?

All these things I just mentioned are extremely important to know in order to have a healthy relationship with anyone. You are basically giving your life away to create a life with a person you are going to live with for the rest of your life. This is extremely serious! Create an inventory of all the questions I just asked and take everything into account. It's better to be safe than sorry.

When you choose to marry someone, you're making a life-or-death decision!

Ana had no idea. Nobody taught her what to look for in a relationship. She didn't see a mature example of a healthy marriage growing up. Her stepfather died when she was nine years old, and her mother's mentality was old- school and naïve when it came to relationships.

As you remember the earlier story Ana shared, Ana's mother married very young, and her first marriage didn't work out. Her second partner was physically abusive and cheated on her multiple times.

She ended up separating from her second partner when Ana was only six years old. Thankfully, Ana doesn't remember how her biological dad was with her mom when he was abusive and toxic. Unfortunately, though, Ana's mother found herself in emotionally abusive relationships on and off.

When Ana's mother was finally in a good relationship on her third try, however, she only had it for a few years because he was tragically killed.

When Ana married her husband, she had only known him for about nine months and the majority of that time was long distance. She didn't know anything about his childhood, his family, his past, or what he wanted for the future. He was a bit shy and didn't share much with anyone. Ana didn't ask questions.

Don't we all do this for the most part when we date? I think we do this because we feel like if we ask deep questions, we are going to make people feel uncomfortable. We need to think differently about this discomfort.

These questions aren't meant to make people feel a certain way about their past. We ask these questions because we need to feel safe, because we deserve honesty, and because we deserve to be in healthy relationships.

According to an article I read from YourDivorce Questions.org, when it comes to first marriages, experts "estimate that 40%-50%" of those marriages will end in divorce or separation.[40] How do we fix this?

I may sound extreme here, but I think that we should talk more about this, and we should create a rule or even a law for anyone who wants to get married to first date each other for a few years and also have them do couple's counseling before getting married.

We might be able to improve these statistics if we were required to date someone for a few years before marriage. Requiring marriage counseling could also help reduce this high rate of divorce.

Why do we continue doing the same thing if we know it has a high rate of not working out? It's time to make a change and start approaching dating and marriage differently.

We need to approach dating and marriage in a healthier way so we can start creating healthy relationships and healthy marriages and healthy families.

In our society, getting married is easy. Nobody asks questions. Everyone is "so happy for you" and they come to your wedding, celebrate, and then they all go home. You sign a legal document that says, "You are husband and wife," congratulations!

Then, when things don't go well and you finally decide you need to get a divorce because your relationship can no longer continue, that's the only time everyone bombards you with questions and tells you what to do. They are in your business, picking sides or trying to keep you together.

You have people from different directions coming at you, making assumptions and thinking that the two people just didn't get along or that they need to get along. Everything becomes overwhelming and stressful.

Even the court, lawyers, and counselors are in your business. The court makes things almost impossible to get a divorce. It all turns into a business deal, benefiting everyone but you. It's all a money business. Our system is broken.

Shouldn't we do it the other way around so our divorce rates won't be as bad as they currently are? I hope that people are more cautious nowadays than they used to be twenty years ago. I really hope things get better and people become wiser and more cautious.

Addictions, Mental Health, Childhood Trauma and the Problems These Issues Bring When We Don't Heal from Them

I have to mention a few things that, unfortunately, not a lot of people talk about. These things are real, confusing, painful, and devastating to many families. It all happens quite often, but for some reason, they still remain hidden and bypassed by society.

Many people choose to keep them secret because of fear or maybe because they feel embarrassed or maybe because they are not familiar with them and they don't know how to approach them.

There are so many relationships that are affected and many couples ultimately end up divorced or separated.

Some people are afflicted by behaviors such as alcoholism, drugs, pornography, food addiction, gambling, mental health problems, and childhood trauma. These issues ruin relationships and split up families. They are hidden, silent killers, and they are extremely disruptive, dysfunctional, confusing, and highly damaging to marriages and families.

What can we do about all these disruptive behaviors that go hidden for many years and nobody thinks about the damage that they create in families and relationships?

Nobody understands the damage they create in relationships and families because nobody wants to talk about them. Only the people who are on the receiving end are the ones who know the stress they go through every day, trying to keep things together. Eventually, they must wake up and let things go, allowing the people who struggle with addictive and destructive behaviors to fix their problems on their own.

The pain and stress their partner goes through is extremely hard and heartbreaking. It's a pain that is often suffered in silence. Everything becomes a daily dysfunction that affects everyone in the family. It corrodes the relationship from the inside out, destroying the relationship emotionally, physically, and financially.

The couple eventually separates or divorces because one person has to care for their partner physically, financially, and emotionally year after year. This type of life is not sustainable. It just doesn't work, no matter how hard you may try.

Even if the couple loves each other deeply, it's not enough because it becomes one-sided. Even when the responsible person tries as hard as possible to do everything to help their partner get up on his/her feet, the relationship just doesn't work in the end.

For a healthy relationship to last, we need both people to be responsible, healthy, and stable, emotionally speaking. All healthy relationships are required to be a two-way relationship.

Both should be uplifting each other, working together towards bettering themselves, relying and trusting each other. Healthy couples are consistent and intentional. They understand the importance of protecting each other and their family, and they make it a purpose to be in tune with each other as they work on building a better future.

There will be moments when one person needs help and their partner will be there to get both up, but that's different. When everything turns into one person constantly lifting up the other person year after year, it becomes taxing and draining.

This is why taking your time getting to know each other during the dating period is so important. Don't get married too soon. Wait until you are in your thirties or even after your thirties. Get to know yourself first. Fall in love with yourself first. Protect yourself.

Another very important thing that happens when you turn thirty is that the brains of most people mature after thirty. This newfound maturity allows you to see life with a different perspective. And with that, you also define your personality a bit more.

Another reason to wait until you are in your thirties is because most people get their personality or behavior more defined after thirty. For example, the onset of mental health illness usually presents itself in the later teenage years through the mid-twenties. A lot of people get married in their twenties, and they are not aware of their partner possibly having mental health problems because the symptoms might be minor at that point. It often takes years for some disorders to present themselves, and by that point, you might have a full-blown mental disaster on your hands.

There are many reasons a person may be having mental health problems at a point in life. Alcohol, drugs, and concussions can hurt your brain. It can create a big problem with your health, and you might be behaving irrationally and not even know the root cause of your behavior.

I personally believe that we should always check our health and do everything we can to heal our emotional and physical traumas.

There is always going to be something that will challenge marriages and relationships, but it is very important to be as mature and healthy as possible before entering a relationship. You should also be very careful because you run the risk of ruining someone's life if you don't take it seriously. Not making wise decisions and jumping into relationships too soon will bring negative consequences.

The Story of Ana and John and How Their Childhood Traumas Negatively Impacted Their Marriage

Ana and John were both young and naïve when they dated each other. They basically did everything old-school.

They met and fell in- love, and just over a few months later, they got married. Most people like Ana and John think, "This is it! I am in love! I am getting married!"

How awesome is that? This is a huge gamble, and it often brings many problems into the relationship. Please don't make this mistake. Take your time to get to know people. Don't jump in right away.

Don't get me wrong—some marriages turn out okay, but the majority of marriages are a big challenge because most people get married without knowing how to have a healthy relationship. When you make a mistake on your own, it's not that big of a deal because you take responsibility for how it affects your life. However, when you're in a relationship, you have to be more cautious so you don't cause problems in your partner's life as well.

When Ana got married, she was excited and had so many dreams and goals for herself and for her marriage. A few months into her marriage, she started noticing that her partner was immature, impulsive, and irrational at times. She didn't understand why. She had no clue what she had gotten herself into.

The man she married was kind, but she soon discovered that something was not right. She couldn't pinpoint the true issues her husband struggled with, nor the reason why he behaved the way he did. His immaturity and inconsistency brought stress, confusion, and frustration to Ana.

They were both in love, young, and naïve about life. They didn't know the importance of being healthy spiritually and emotionally speaking. He had childhood traumas and insecurities that Ana didn't know about. All Ana knew about her husband was that he was sweet, kind, and a Christian man. That was all Ana could see, and that meant everything to her.

We all have childhood traumas and insecurities, but some have more than others. We need to remember that it is not what happens to us that's important, but what we do with those experiences. We must find a way to heal and overcome our hardships.

For Ana's husband, the childhood traumas destroyed his confidence before he even knew what confidence and self-love meant. John told Ana his experience growing up with a father who was verbally and physically abusive and a mother who was emotionally absent.

I can't imagine the life of Ana's husband as a child. To have a mother that, even though was physically there, was not emotionally present and to have a father who was verbally aggressive and physically abusive can be emotionally and mentally traumatizing.

This type of upbringing can be mind- altering because when you grow up in an environment of fear, you automatically are going to be in a state of fight, flight, or freeze mode. You are going to be in survival mode. There is no room for feeling safe or loved when you operate in fear.

The two most important things a child needs are LOVE and Safety. Unfortunately, he didn't have that. It was very hard for Ana to see her husband unable to love or believe in himself. She saw so much potential in her husband, but unfortunately, he didn't see it. He didn't know how to see his potential or how to use it. He learned—little by little—later in life through Ana's help.

If we don't have a foundation of love or safety, we suffer and live with so much confusion, insecurities, and pain, and we end up hurting the people we love. It is very sad to know that there are so many people living their lives without being loved or feeling safe.

True love, compassion, and empathy start with yourself, but when you don't see it modeled in childhood, you don't understand it. If we don't have a foundation of self-love and if we don't have the ability to self-regulate, it can be very hard to have a healthy relationship with others.

Remember, you cannot give what you don't have. When we carry emotional trauma, we don't see things as they are; we see things as we are. If a person hurts inside, they automatically think the people around them are the problem. Hurt people hurt people, and they often like to blame others for their circumstances.

They also disconnect from the ability to understand their true purpose in life. When people are hurting and lack the ability to self- regulate, they often like to play the victim because that's the easiest and safest place for them. They use that as a coping mechanism. Playing the victim blocks you from seeing the reality of things and, unfortunately, you cannot grow when you don't take full responsibility for yourself.

Ana's relationship with her husband became toxic as she tried to understand him and help him work through his emotions. She didn't know she was dealing with something very serious and extremely stressful. Her husband's problem grew much bigger than Ana was prepared for.

She basically became her husband's therapist and coach. As time went on, Ana felt emotionally drained, disappointed, alone, unhappy, and resentful toward her husband and even towards God. Remember back to the time when Ana prayed for her future husband? Ana thought because she prayed for it, God would make it happen. When it didn't, Ana felt confused and disappointed. This is our human nature, but God operates in different ways and his ways are always perfect, even when we don't understand them.

It was hard for Ana to see her husband's emotions going up and down almost daily. It was sad, draining, confusing, and frustrating for her. But, despite these feelings, Ana still hoped her husband would heal and become the man God created him to be. She wanted her husband to be a stable husband who was emotionally steady, healthy, and financially secure.

As she went through the challenges over several years, she kept asking God, "Why did you allow me to get into this situation? I prayed, and I really thought this was your will. Why does this feel so confusing? I'm doing everything to help him. What am I learning from this? I'm praying for my husband. I'm being supportive of him emotionally, physically, and financially. What else am I supposed to do? Why do I feel stuck? Why do I feel like he drags me down? It doesn't feel like a fair connection. Something is not right here.

What is my purpose in this relationship? I feel like you gave me the bad end of the stick with this marriage. I prayed for my husband, and I believed you would bless me with a "good husband". Why is he not mature and emotionally healthy? Is this what a marriage is supposed to look like or feel like? How do I pray? How do I believe? I don't even know what do believe anymore. I'm confused.

This relationship feels exhausting and unfair on so many levels. I don't understand what your purpose for me in this relationship is. I don't see your point, God.

You see, Ana was wrestling with God and doubting her journey. She had the right to ask all these questions. After all, how do we find the answers if we don't ask all the questions necessary as we go through challenges in life? God is so good and gentle with us and he allows us to question everything as we go through challenging times in life. Even in our struggles, he is still holding us in the palm of his hand.

All we need to do is trust him and push through our journeys with dignity and honor, no matter how hard the trials may be at times. He knows that as we endure our challenges, we will always rise up, and only then we will see and discover our purpose. Only when you gain strength and rise up, you are able to see your true calling in life.

Ana didn't know she took on a burden that didn't belong to her. It was not Ana's responsibility to heal her husband. However, it was her husband's responsibility to heal himself so he could become the best version of himself. There were many times where Ana felt like leaving the relationship because her husband didn't work on himself. Things would go from being good for a little while and then things would go back to being dysfunctional and confusing again. The relationship became codependent.

Ana didn't know that by constantly coming to her husband's rescue, she ended up enabling him without even knowing what she was doing. Her husband John ended up not working as hard on himself because he knew Ana would come to the rescue every time he needed help or got in trouble, physically or financially speaking. She was always helping him fix his problems.

The combination of Ana and John's personalities created a perfect match for codependency because he was broken inside and needed what Ana subconsciously gave in her relationships. Ana's need to care for others worked like a magnet on John. Ana was broken as well. Her need to help was not healthy either, because she didn't realize she was hurting herself by constantly coming to the rescue and solving her husband's problems.

She didn't know how to get out of the relationship and let her husband make mistakes and assume the consequences of his mistakes. Ana felt like she couldn't let go because she didn't want John to hurt any more than he already was. She wanted to protect her husband and felt obligated to help him and keep things together. Could Ana's need to rescue and protect her husband have to do with the fact that she couldn't rescue her stepfather from being killed? I would say so.

Ana also had a lot of childhood traumas she needed to heal from in herself. When we go through life and don't learn to heal from our traumas, even the ones we are not aware of, we end up creating more problems because we try to compensate. We create coping mechanisms.

We try to find happiness in our brokenness; we try to find happiness in people or things, but our true happiness is not in anything outside of us. True happiness is found within us as we learn to heal our wounds, as we accept ourselves and as we learn to love and accept our creator, regardless of what we go through in life.

Ana's marriage was a learning experience. She took on many responsibilities that belonged to her husband. It was her husband's responsibility to heal his childhood and emotional traumas. It was emotionally draining for Ana to have to feel responsible for her husband's emotions and having to guide him and teach him how to be responsible. It was dysfunctional.

This is usually what ends up happening in most marriages when they get married too young and when they don't have the right guidance or knowledge of what makes healthy marriages. Ana and John were both twenty- three years old when they got married. At times, he was needy and more of an emotional burden to Ana, rather than a healthy and supportive partner.

Ana didn't know what to do. She loved her husband, but she knew deep in her heart that it was time for her to stand her ground, let go of the responsibilities that didn't belong to her, and focus on her own healing journey.

She realized she was becoming emotionally and physically ill after all the years she took on the responsibility of her husband's childhood traumas and irresponsible behavior.

Ana found herself with extreme stress and anxiety, which often gets overlooked. Women are natural caretakers and fixers. We want to make things better for everyone, but we often forget ourselves and our needs, and in the end, we feel exhausted and emotionally drained because most of our energy goes toward helping others. I also want to add that men experience relationships like this as well, and they also go through what Ana went through. This can happen to anyone.

Eventually, this constant caretaking puts us in situations that make us sick. As soon as we realize what made us sick to begin with, we start taking action by prioritizing ourselves over others, and we begin to feel much better.

You will disappoint people, however, when you stand up for yourself and say no. Don't allow that disappointment to guilt-trip you into turning your back on yourself; those other people are not your responsibility. Besides, who will you be able to help if your stress and anxiety get so bad that it puts you on your deathbed?

Sometimes, when you get into these situations, you might be tempted to call your doctor for anti-depression or anti-anxiety meds.

We are also going to disappoint people when we decide to say no and separate ourselves from people and things that are not healthy for our mental and emotional well- being.

The majority of times, we don't need medication. We need to heal ourselves through prayer, meditation and a healthy lifestyle first. Start with holistic medicine if you feel you need a doctor. We start by working on healing our childhood and emotional traumas.

We all know that sometimes Western medicine will be needed. It is great for certain things, but should only be used if you really need to. For instance, it can be helpful if you break your leg or need surgery, but not for emotional trauma. When we feel emotionally sick, depressed, or anxious, we should always seek holistic methods, therapy, meditation, exercise, and healthy foods.

Highly processed foods can also cause your body to be depressed, believe it or not.[41] When you eat highly processed foods, it disrupts your gut microbiome. When you have an unhealthy gut microbiome, your brain won't function properly.

Stress will also disrupt your gut microbiome. When you have too much stress, even if you eat healthy, your body will still feel sick.

Every time Ana went to her doctors, they offered her muscle relaxers, anti-anxiety medication, antidepressants and so on. She never took the medication because she knew it would add more problems before it helped her solve the current one. Ana didn't want to end up with a side effect of any medication her body didn't need. In her mind, she knew she needed to dig deep into what was causing her the extreme stress, anxiety, and depression. She was protective of her body, and if she had to take medication for anything, she would go to holistic resources as her primary option.

Ana was on constant stress for so many years that she became hyper-vigilant. She didn't know how to rest. She felt like if she relaxed, something bad would happen. The environment she was in for many years didn't allow her to relax and let go of worries. She developed PTSD. She kept it in because she felt she had to be strong, but it started showing through her constant worried and hyper- vigilant behavior.

In 2022, Ana was diagnosed with anxiety and depression. She had anxiety and depression for years before she finally accepted the diagnosis and allowed her new doctor to help her. Her new doctor was wise and decided to connect her with a therapist who worked on helping her heal her emotional traumas. She told Ana that she didn't need to take medication because her anxiety and depression were environmental and not due to her biology. Ana was willing to work with her new doctor because she didn't push any pills on her. She truly cared and did things in a holistic way.

Ana felt as though her doctor and her therapist were her angels, helping her relieve her trauma and helping her restore herself by talking to her therapist and doing exercises that helped her heal naturally with no medication.

Ana's homework from her therapist was to create a journal and write down all the feelings and frustrations she had bottled up inside and to create an environment of rest. To slow down and to pamper herself. To allow herself to receive. To allow others to take care of her. She did her meditation and deep breathing exercises almost religiously.

A study by WebMD says, "Both depression and anxiety are very common, and they often happen together. About 60% of people with anxiety also have symptoms of depression, and vice versa."[42] "It can be harder for doctors to diagnose and treat depression and anxiety when they happen together. That's why it's important to tell your doctor about all of your symptoms."[43]

Whatever you go through or whatever you are feeling, if you ever experience anxiety or depression at some point in your life, my advice to you is please don't reach for the pill right away. Our human nature is to look for the quick fix, but that will always bring side effects of some sort. Look inward and see if you can heal yourself as you heal your emotional trauma or fix your environmental stressors. Do the work and truly take care of yourself. Nurture yourself.

We need to be able to be aware of our stressors and our emotional traumas, and we need to be able to tackle them in a healthy way with healthy healing resources in order for us to truly heal from the inside out.

Our bodies will always tell us when something is not right in our spirit or when something is not right with our emotions. Instead of reaching out for a quick fix or a superficial resource to fix our problems, listen to your body.

Thankfully, Ana can say now that she is on a beautiful path of healing and wholeness. She is on a path of strength, and she wants to give back by helping others achieve their healing journeys.

Ana's story is a perfect example of healing from the inside out. Also, please don't forget that healing is an individual process. Ana has been dedicated to her healing journey. She is willing to keep consistent, and she has chosen to share the raw parts of her life because she knows that only through our imperfections are we able to examine our lives and gain strength to work on healing ourselves.

Denial is your enemy. You will not heal if you are in denial. It's like trying to cover the sun with one finger. It just never works. If you are serious about healing and becoming the best version of yourself, allow yourself to be raw and honest with yourself.

No matter what I tell you, if you are not ready to start your healing journey, you will not heal. However, Ana was ready to finally heal herself. She worked on her healing journey every day and night because she got to the point of being sick and tired of being sick and tired. Ana also wanted to live her life with a purpose.

The healing process for Ana's husband had to happen on his time because he wasn't ready at the same time Ana was ready to heal. It was not an easy process for Ana, but it was worth it. So, after thirteen years, Ana decided to leave the relationship and create a safe environment for herself and her children. She realized she could not do the work for him to heal.

He had to take his physical and emotional health very seriously if he really wanted to heal and be healthy from the inside out. Even though Ana was out of the relationship, she still helped John get to the root of his self- destructive and unhealthy behavior. She knew that something was not right in his brain because he was trying hard to be stable and healthy, but he was not able to control his behavior.

Ana took John to Amen's Clinic for a brain SPECT imaging (single-photon emission computerized tomography). This machine is a 3D brain mapping tool that gives doctors more information so they can diagnose their patients more effectively. Through brain SPECT imaging, doctors can see the blood flow and activity of the brain.

Dr. Amen has several clinics throughout the U.S. He is extremely knowledgeable and he truly cares for his patients. His love and dedication have brought hope and healing to many people.

(This is not a paid advertisement. Dr. Amen does not know I am writing this book. I am choosing to share about the amazing impact he has made in my life and in the lives of many of my friends and family. He has changed people's lives throughout the course of his career.)

I am sharing this information only because I believe many people will benefit from it. I want to bring awareness and healing to as many people as possible. It brought so much healing and clarity to Ana and John.

When Ana called to make an appointment, they were very helpful, and they immediately made an appointment for John the next day. It was a blessing in disguise for Ana and John.

Dr. Amen is an amazing doctor with a strong intuition and knowledge when it comes to healing the brain. The way he examines the brain is how all doctors should examine the brain before giving any diagnosis to anybody.

I agree 100 percent with what Dr. Amen says about the brain and our bodies. Dr. Amen says the brain is the only part of the body that psychiatrists diagnose without even looking at it. How can this be possible?

Why do we scan everything else in our bodies before diagnosing anything, and why do we bypass the brain when our brains are what control our bodies? If we don't have healthy brains, we cannot have healthy bodies or healthy lives.

Dr. Amen has saved so many lives and helped heal so many families. His knowledge, compassion, and dedication have helped many families get their lives back to normal. He is a Godsend.

Dr. Amen was the answer to Ana's prayers. Ana wanted to know if the issues John was having were due to his brain injuries, or maybe it was a combination of his childhood traumas and his brain injuries.

At this point, John was willing to do anything to heal himself, because he knew deep in his heart that he needed to heal his mind and body and because he knew that no matter where he went, if he didn't heal himself, his life was never going to be normal and stable. An unhealthy lifestyle is never sustainable.

Because he knew his behavior was not sustainable no matter where he went in life, he made it a purpose to get better. Ana made the decision to move on and protect herself, even though she was still helping John. She knew it was time for her to start her healing journey.

Ana had to be intentional and emotionally strong to focus on a journey of healing and internal peace. If she didn't leave, she would also be inconsistent with the person she wanted to be. John's poor life choices affected her entirely, no matter how hard she tried to be stable and to create a stable environment for herself and her family. It was like trying to climb a slippery hill. No matter how hard she tried, she still ended up at the bottom, having to start over. She was tired of her life being all over the place.

Ana ended up feeling like she didn't belong anywhere. She felt confused and depressed because of what she went through. On top of that, her experiences weren't easy to talk about, so she had to keep them buried inside for a long time. This was an invisible problem sabotaging her life and her future plans. It was robbing her of her peace in her life.

When Ana took John to Amen's clinics to get a brain scan, she told the doctors, "Please make sure to do everything you can. Please check everything to make sure we know exactly what he has so that we can fix it if we can."

John had a brain SPECT. The results of John's brain scan showed he had a few concussions growing up that caused a chemical imbalance. One major concussion happened during his college years, when he was riding a motorcycle and lost control. He ended up unconscious on the street for a while, then woke up in the ambulance, not knowing why he was there. It took him a few months to recover from that accident. He also had another motorcycle accident a couple months after he and Ana got married.

She only dated John for about nine months, and the majority of those months were long- distance, so she was not able to fully know him. Because everything was beautiful and exciting at first, she felt as though marrying John was the right thing to do. Back then, Ana was young and in love, and after she got married, she thought she would have an amazing marriage. Ana had dreams and expectations for herself and her husband, but she didn't know her life was going to take a turn in the wrong direction.

Life is full of challenges, and the only thing we can do is live life one day at a time and remind ourselves that we can rise up and heal, no matter what life throws at us. Remember that as long as we are alive, we have a calling, and we have the ability to become better and not bitter. We can be a ray of hope in this world.

Sometimes bad things are going to happen, and we are not going to have control over that, but the most important thing we can do is to stay firm and consistent and do our best to be gentle with ourselves and our loved ones. Only God knows why some people go through more challenges than others.

One week before Ana and John's wedding, John's dad passed away. He had battled cancer for several years. Somehow, he knew he would not make it, so he called John and Ana and told them to go ahead and get married no matter what happened to him.

Unfortunately, he passed away. It was hard for John and Ana to go through a happy moment and sad moment all at the same time. These kinds of emotions must be processed and healed, otherwise they get trapped inside of us and come out in unhealthy ways.

A few days after the death of his dad, Ana noticed that John was not being himself. Ana thought, "Maybe he is hurting inside and doesn't know how to mourn the death of his dad."

He didn't know how to express his feelings and regulate his emotions. Ana was surprised when he didn't show any emotion. She was surprised to see that he didn't share how he felt about his dad or how he felt about his dad's death. She was also surprised to see or learn that he didn't have a very close relationship with the rest of his family.

A few weeks went by after their wedding as Ana continued to learn about John and his lack of emotional expression. He was hurting inside, but he didn't know how to express his emotions. He would behave irrationally, and he would throw temper tantrums like a toddler might. It was very confusing for Ana to see the behavior that would come out of the man she married.

After a few months in their marriage, John had another motorcycle accident. John's behavior continued to escalate. He was reckless and inconsistent. It was very hard for the people who knew him to see that something was off, but they could not pinpoint the root cause.

Childhood traumas and brain injuries are very hard to diagnose without proper examination, and many people are often misdiagnosed. It is very sad. This has to change. Ana went through hell and back all because she just didn't know how to help John or who to take him to, to get him healed.

It took Ana thirteen years to figure out what the problem was and how to find the solution to help John start his healing journey. She was physically exhausted and emotionally drained. She took on so much responsibility she didn't even know she wasn't supposed to take on.

Ana felt responsible for him because if she didn't help him, nobody else would. She tried reaching out to his family, but they were in denial. They never helped. His family ignored everything Ana tried to share with them. They were disrespectful, and they didn't believe that something was seriously wrong with John.

They hardly ever visited Ana and John, so they were completely unaware of John's behavior. In the thirteen years of Ana and John's marriage, his family only visited twice. And every time they visited, they refused to see the truth.

They were emotionally detached from each other, and they were also critical and judgmental towards Ana. Ana made a choice to not talk to his family because they were no help whatsoever. She just didn't want to bother calling them.

Ana had to do the healing process on her own and ignore his family or anyone who was not helping. She had to create an environment of healing for herself, her children, and John.

She was still carrying all the weight and responsibility, as she was trying her best to let go of John. She managed her challenges as kindly as possible and as patiently as possible because she truly cared about John and his wellbeing.

Even though John's family didn't help, there were others who were there for both Ana and John. Ana's close friends and friends from church would call and give Ana emotional support. They would also call John to check on him and also to keep him accountable.

When John started his healing journey, he didn't know how to start. He was resistant, and he would go from working on healing to rebelling against what was healthy for his brain and body.

Concussions are mind-altering, but thankfully, we can restore our brains as we nourish them. Did you know our brain cells can regenerate? Yes, there is hope! We can restore our brain cells and our health, but we need to be consistent and intentional with our health.

John didn't have a healthy diet, and he was resistant to Ana's healthy eating suggestions. He was in denial. The main work he needed to do was to heal his emotions and childhood traumas. He needed to believe in himself and believe he was worthy of being and feeling healthy. John also needed to learn he had the power within himself to renew and restore his emotional and physical health.

He didn't know he could heal and restore his brain and his emotions by changing his lifestyle, meditating for clarity, and working through his childhood traumas. It all sounds easy, but these are the hardest things to do, but worth doing it. In the end, we are transformed into beautiful and emotionally healthy people.

Ana was a very intuitive person. She knew deep in her heart that making healthy changes could heal anyone. Prayer and meditation were very important for Ana. That's how she could cope with everything she went through with John and help him start his own healing journey.

John, at some point, became self- destructive and resistant to his doctor's healthy eating suggestions. His health got worse due to his negative thoughts and his unhealthy eating habits.

When John saw his brain test results, it was an epiphany for him. He realized he had to take serious actions to heal his body and restore his brain.

He started taking action to heal and restore his brain. It was not easy in the beginning for him. He didn't know how to love or take care of himself. He worked on building that foundation through Ana's help and support.

Even though Ana was focusing on herself and created healthy boundaries between them, she was still there to help him. She still chose to stick around and encourage him and help him with his eating habits, exercising, meditation practices, and prayer.

Ana was his support emotionally, spiritually, and physically. John often says that without her help, he "would have ended up in a deep, dark place" in his life.

Ana followed the advice of several doctors and psychologists for many years. She learned so much from them, and their teachings helped her heal herself and helped her guide John on the right path for him to start his healing journey.

Some of the amazing people she listened to religiously were Dr. Joe Dispenza, Dr. Amen and his wife Tana Amen, Dr. Wayne W. Dyer, Bruce Lipton, Anita Moorjani, John and Lisa Bevere, and Vishen Lakhiani.

All these amazing people have impacted Ana's life miraculously. I have the blessing to know her personally because I am her. I had to keep my name out throughout the story because when I started writing my story I couldn't get it out in words.

It was too painful to share so I had to make myself a third party in order to see my story with different eyes. I am thankful for all the trials I went through. The trials I went through helped me learn a lot about myself. I learned to heal my own childhood traumas, and I learned to heal others through my personal experience and wisdom.

The pain and trials I went through in life made me who I am now. I see life with love, and I have compassion for myself and others. My life is joyful, and I live with gratitude, and purpose every day.

You see, when you gain and share knowledge, you can make a positive impact on the lives of others. Don't be afraid to share your story. Somebody out there needs to hear your story. Your story has the power to heal and empower others.

Little by little, John started understanding how to heal and the importance of love (self-love) and self-care. John also took responsibility for his actions. Ana was so proud of him for taking action on working on his healing journey. Ana kept him accountable. He saw the big difference that prayer, meditation and eating healthy could make. It felt like a miracle was happening in his and Ana's lives.

John started taking responsibility for his actions. Ana did everything to help him heal. She helped him heal through healthy food, meditation, heathy habits, and prayer. Prayer is powerful.

After a while, Ana saw a new and healthy person in John. As John worked on his healing journey, Ana was able to have mature conversations with him without him being argumentative or irrational in his actions. John saw with clarity that his life was changing for the better as he made healthy choices to nourish his mind, body, and soul.

Even though John was working toward healing his mind and body, there were days where he did great, and there were days where his behavior went back to his old habits. It was an everyday challenge. It was extremely hard and draining for Ana to see John going through a rollercoaster of emotions as he tried to heal and as he tried to understand his journey.

She loved him and she wanted more than anything in the world for him to be healthy. Ana also wanted their lives to be stable and "normal"—that is, if there's such a thing as normal. She didn't know what was normal anymore, but she knew something was not right. The way John lived his life was not sustainable, no matter how hard Ana tried.

Ana was a person who liked everything in order. She was a planner, worked hard at everything she did, and had high expectations of herself and her partner. John was the opposite of Ana.

He didn't want to be the way he was. Deep in his heart, he wanted everything Ana wanted, but he didn't know how to obtain it. He struggled with believing that he could be healed and that he didn't have to live a dysfunctional life. It was exhausting even for him. He had a lot to work on and learn from in order to create healthy habits.

As John continued to learn how to eat healthy and how to be transparent with himself, little by little, he understood that he could heal himself as he worked through his childhood traumas. He also learned to discipline himself as he embraced healthy eating habits and mindfulness meditation to heal himself from the inside out.

Thanks to Dr. Joe Dispenza's YouTube meditation videos and all the healing videos Ana shared with him almost every day, John learned to heal his childhood traumas, and he learned to rewire his brain. It was like a healing miracle started to unfold.

We cannot create a healthy future if we continue falling back into our old habits or our old ways of thinking. We are what we think, and we are our daily habits, whether they are healthy or unhealthy. The choice will always be up to us.

As Dr. Joe Dispenza says in his book titled You Are the Placebo:

"Your personality is made up of how you think, act, and feel. It is your state of being. Therefore, your same thoughts, actions, and feelings will keep you enslaved to the same past personal reality. However, when you as a personality embrace new thoughts, actions, and feelings, you will inevitably create a new personal reality in your future."[44]

When we come to the realization of what is causing our bodies and minds to be dysfunctional and make a conscious decision to change that part of us, that is when we start working toward healing our psychological traumas, our pains, and hurts.

It is not an easy journey. It takes consistency. It takes self-love and self- discipline. It takes courage. It takes determination. It takes anger, the righteous anger. It takes getting to the point of being sick and tired of being sick and tired, and I mean being sick and tired of living lives that no longer serve us. Lives that put us in a lower state of mind. Lives that hurt us rather than inspire us and elevate us.

When we continue to make toxic decisions, we continue creating lives that blind us and take us away from who we are meant to be in this world. We all have a calling and a reason to live in this world.

We can only make positive changes when we are willing to be raw and honest with ourselves. It requires us to be transparent about our thoughts and let go of our old programming.

When we become aware of the power within us and the emotional and spiritual blockages in our minds, bodies and spirits, only then can we start our healing journey.

We all have a strong power or strong powers within us. When we allow the lies of society and even our own lies to control us, and when we allow denial into our lives, it hinders us. It paralyzes us. It numbs us. It blocks us from becoming the best versions of ourselves.

Ana and John loved each other deeply, and even though Ana was always there for John, she was ready and at peace with herself by letting go so she could start a new and healthy path. Ana felt the need to let go because she needed stability, peace, and calm in her life. She focused on creating that for herself. Her priority was herself and her children. She was happy within herself.

John worked hard to become the best version of himself. It was a work in progress. Ana had to let go so John could take full responsibility to heal himself. Only when you take responsibility for yourself is when you can transform yourself. Nobody can do the full healing for you because healing is a personal responsibility. As the old saying goes, "You can lead the horse to water but you can't make him drink."

Ana truly hoped John would take full responsibility for himself and become the best version of himself, no matter where he went. She hoped that he would become fully healthy, but that, only the future would tell.

As Ana and John learned to heal their emotions, traumas, and pain, they became stronger and healthier individually and as a family. She focused on her inner peace and purpose in life, and she became the best version of herself. Ana felt FREE and empowered within herself.

John embraced Ana's advice for healing as he discovered that meditation and prayer and living a healthy lifestyle were helping him become the best version of himself.

Ana had given John all the necessary tools to heal himself and renew his mind and become the best version of himself. It was up to John to heal from within.

Only when you are ready to make a true change within yourself is when you will be able to let go of the old habits and old mindset.

Nobody can make that change for you. It's a personal experience and a personal responsibility. Each of us can become anything we want, but this only happens according to each individual's timing and the work we are willing to do.

Will John truly keep consistent and continue the work toward his healing to become the best version of himself? We do not know if John will continue his journey of healing, but Ana hoped with all her heart he would be consistent and become the best example for his children and the generations to follow. At the end of the day, it is not what happens to us that's important, but what we do with it. We need to find a way to leave a legacy of honor and encouragement to those who come after us.

God is good, and his plans are always better than our plans. All we need to do is to be true to ourselves, trust our intuition, and do the work within ourselves. When we do the deep work within ourselves, it shows on the outside. It shows as we speak and handle ourselves. It shows as we respect ourselves and others. And it shows as we respect life and accept our journeys.

Ana's favorite words are, "Whether you do or not, it will show," and, "We cannot fake our inner healing." She was true to herself and transparent with God as she struggled with the trials of life. No matter what she faced, she didn't let go of her hope, and she didn't let go of her faith.

She endured a lot of pain, confusion, and disappointment in her life and in her relationship with John due to his childhood trauma, but she would always see the positive in everything. Ana accepted her journey as she gave her all to help John heal. She thought she was doing the work to help John heal, and she did, but she also healed herself throughout the process.

Her resilience, compassion, and bravery helped her endure the trials she had in life and in her marriage. She had wisdom and empathy for others. John was thankful for her in his life.

John wrote a message to Ana:

Thank you from the bottom of my heart for all that you have done for me and for our family. I could have ended up as just another statistic and broken from emotional traumas and brain injuries, but thanks to your wisdom, dedication, resilience, intuition, compassion, and bravery, I was able to heal and I am now able to be the best version of myself. God's love and wisdom through you taught me how to love myself and, in return, be capable of truly loving you in a healthy way. I love you now more than when we first got married. You are a woman with wisdom. You are my rock and my compass. I have a new beginning in my life now and there is so much good that is starting to happen because of you. Keep shining as a bright beacon of hope to those around you! You are my forever love and I am truly blessed to have you in my life!

"And we know that in all things God works for good for those who love him, who have been called according to his purpose." Romans 8:28.

Love,
John

Life is beautiful, no matter how messy it may feel at times. You can always rise up and healing and wholeness will come through, as long as you stay grounded and true to yourself.

Ana had strong intuition and her faith helped her make wise decisions in her life. She wasn't perfect, but she knew her faith and intuition were her guides in her journey.

She was also willing to be true to herself and vulnerable with herself. When you are true and vulnerable with yourself, you can do anything. Miracles will happen.

Ana used a very famous prayer on the back of her wedding invitations without even knowing she was really going to need it on her journey with John. The song is titled "The Prayer", which is sung by Celine

Dion and Andrea Bocelli and was originally written by Carole Bayer Sager and David Foster. Many of you know it. If you don't know it, please look it up on the internet. I could not put the lyrics here because I don't own the rights to them.

Ana was in awe when she realized that the words in that prayer held so much truth in her journey. She truly needed God's eyes, wisdom, and grace in order to ride the wave of confusion and frustration in her marriage.

God's plans are always better than our plans. Through God's wisdom, we can rise above our circumstances.

We all need this prayer in our lives. We all struggle with something one way or another. Nobody has it easy. If you are breathing, you will have challenges at some point in your life.

My advice to you is to nurture your intuition and self-love. Never let go of it. Don't let society rob you of your intuition and self-love. Your intuition is your wisdom, your gut feeling. We were all born with it.

We can develop our intuition as we look deep into ourselves, meditate, quiet our minds, and ask our creator to give us wisdom. This deep work will reveal the parts we need to work on so we can see beyond our human ability and understanding.

I hope you take time to quiet all the noise that distracts you and allow yourself to meditate and start your healing journey. I hope that you take time to love and nurture yourself. Allow yourself to become a new you and be a gift to others.

Hurt People, Addictions, and Codependency

Trauma creates more trauma, and "hurt people hurt people." We've all heard this phrase before. Codependency is a toxic pattern that is hard to break out of. If we don't work on healing our emotional traumas and our old self-programming, we will live our lives masking ourselves and pretending to be healthy. This way of living is never sustainable because it hurts your potential. It hurts your future, and it hurts your loved ones.

When we live our lives in denial of our emotions and traumas, we do a great disservice to our potentially healed future selves. We can also hurt those around us. We hold ourselves back, and we also hold our loved ones back.

Any emotional or physical trauma or addiction will destroy your relationships, even if you try very hard to maintain them. When you are not healthy, you cannot be the best version of yourself nor give the best version of yourself to your loved ones.

You might try to be good for a few days. You might think that you are able to quit your unhealthy habits and addictions such as alcoholism, pornography, lying, cheating, excessive shopping, bad eating habits, laziness. I can go on and on, but if you don't have a support system, and if you are not honest, if you are not transparent, if you lack integrity. If you don't have self-love and self- discipline, your behavior will go back to the old habits and toxic mechanisms. This way of living will always keep you up and down, and nothing you do will ever be stable and fruitful.

These issues I mentioned above, unfortunately, happen to many relationships and families. When it comes to trauma and hurt, we all struggle. When you to deal with your partner's dysfunctional behaviors and addictions, you may think you're helping, but you will always end up holding yourself back and living in constant stress. It is a toxic environment, and it's important to recognize it and put a stop to it if you want to live healthily in a healthy environment.

For people to become healthy, they need to become aware of their unhealthy patterns and their toxic behaviors. Awareness is everything. It's actually the first step to our transformations. John's immature choices brought emotional and financial problems into the relationship. He had to become aware of what was affecting his life and his responsibilities as a man, and Ana needed to stop enabling him. We cannot grow if we don't take responsibility for our health and our actions.

When it comes to healthy and thriving relationships, it takes two people who are aware of their emotional traumas and willing to heal and lead healthier lives. When you are in a relationship, make sure to see how your energy is being used.

When you carry hurt and trauma, you will continue to fall into dysfunctional relationships. You will continue to have negativity in your life. This type of negative environment will take away your joy and happiness. We are humans, and we will have problems and disagreements here and there, but it should not be a constant distraction in your relationship or in your personal growth.

If your energy is being used in a negative environment and you feel more drained than elevated and re-energized, you are probably in the wrong relationship. No relationship is worth your energy when you feel emotionally drained, confused, and stuck.

Reevaluate yourself, your desires, and goals. If you both have driven personalities, understand the value of working in harmony with each other, and elevate each other. Your relationship will have a greater chance of survival.

When people are hurting and broken, they continue to hurt others, and their problem continues growing until one decides to put a stop to it.

For example, in Ana's story. Even though she went through times of confusion and disappointments in her childhood and through her relationship, she learned and grew tremendously. She didn't stay stuck. Her husband's unstable patterns actually helped her see the true problem and the solution as clear as water.

Once she could pinpoint the true problems in her relationship, she took action and worked on establishing healthy boundaries. When she was able to break her need to enable her husband's unhealthy patterns, things started to change. She felt like she could breathe; she felt free and empowered.

John understood what he needed to do, and he was on board with Ana. It was not easy at first because they both had to work on their hurts and unhealthy and familiar patterns. John knew he couldn't build a stable life until he took care of his childhood traumas and let go of his demons.

No matter what you go through in life, nobody is responsible for you. Nobody is responsible for your health. Nobody is responsible for your success. The responsibility falls 100 percent on you.

I am not here to tell you what to do. You are free to do what you think is best for you. The only thing I can say is to take care of yourself and don't let anything or anyone rob you of your joy and true calling. I also want you to dig deep into your problems. Ask a lot of questions. Don't stay stuck. Free yourself and heal any emotional trauma you may be carrying.

Life is not easy, and relationships can be taxing. Love yourself and make sure you are emotionally healed, so when you get into a relationship, you can recognize any red flags and do what is best for you before you get too deep into it.

Believe it or not, this happens quite often to many women who find themselves in relationships with dysfunctional men who are in denial of their childhood traumas and addictions.

It's important to remember it's not only men who are dysfunctional and emotionally unstable. This can happen to anyone and in any relationship. The purpose of me sharing this with you is so I can create awareness and for you to start thinking and analyzing your relationship with your partner.

If it's dysfunctional, it might be time to let go, or it might be time to start working on yourself and start healing your traumas, addictions, or anything blocking you from being a healthy partner.

No relationship should feel like you have to carry all the burden. No relationship should make you feel anxious, stressed out, or like you don't belong anywhere. It shouldn't make you feel lonely and depressed. It shouldn't make you feel physically sick.

Dysfunctional people who have problems with addictions, traumas, or unhealthy behaviors can become healthy. There is hope for everyone, but they need to be willing to be transparent and honest with their emotions and traumas to start healing.

These people have two choices in life. Number one, they can give excuses as to why they have no control over their childhood emotional traumas or their addictions and will continue to play the victim as they mask their problems, or number two, they will not give excuses and will confront their demons to start their healing journeys. Only then will they start making a positive impact on their lives, marriages, relationships, and families.

When Ana drew the line with John, took action to focus on herself, and did what was best for her, John was willing to work on healing his childhood trauma and making healthy choices. It took him this long to start making healthy choices. Why did it take him this long? Maybe he was forced to take responsibility because his enabler was not willing to continue the toxic and dysfunctional pattern.

This is how you stop unhealthy patterns. This is how you start your healing journey. This is how you heal your past generational traumas and, ultimately, this is how you heal your next generation. Be brave. Be willing. Be transparent. Be vulnerable.

Be kind to one another and be considerate of others. In this world, everyone is fighting a battle you know nothing about. Be the wisdom and hope for someone else during their storm. Bring hope, love, and healing to yourself and others. Be the sunshine in someone's darkness.

Sexual Abuse, Sexual Molestation, and Sexual Harassment

Nobody wants to talk about sexual abuse. Unfortunately, there are no laws that do full justice when it comes to these types of abuse, and I include sexual molestation and sexual harassment because, in my own opinion, they create mental and emotional trauma in the victim. However, according to the law, sexual molestation or sexual harassment are not categorized as sexual abuse, and there are no consequences for sexual molestation. I spoke with a friend of mine who is a prosecuting attorney regarding this subject, and here is what he told me: "The only way to press charges is if there is physical evidence." This is devastating and humiliating.

What about the emotional and mental trauma that a child must deal with for the rest of his/her life? A child who has been molested has been robbed of his/her innocence and ability to trust anyone. It brings shame, confusion, and pain. A child who has been molested is never the same. Some fall into deep depression, and some even end up committing suicide.

It is extremely frustrating that the current laws do not back anyone who has been sexually abused, molested, or sexually harassed. No wonder so many people whose children have been molested take matters into their own hands.

This is very unfortunate, and it can be fixed if we are brave enough to talk about it, stand up against it, and take action to change the laws. We are in desperate need of better laws when it comes to these issues. Please keep in mind that the only way to change our current laws is when we speak up. We must be brave and speak up. Nothing will change unless we speak up.

A very sad and tragic truth is that one in three children does not disclose their abuser until they are an adult. Most children and women are forced to keep their trauma in silence because of fear, confusion, and shame.

According to RAINN, "Every 68, seconds an American is sexually assaulted."[45] Also, "93% of child victims know their perpetrator."[46] This is definitely not a stranger danger thing whatsoever, and it needs to be addressed. The majority of sex offenders are family members. This is devastating, and it is pure evil. Abuse and shame abide in silence. We cannot keep silent.

"On average, there are 463,634 victims (ages 12 or older) of sexual violence each year" in the United States."[47]

We have to do something to change the laws, but how do we change these laws? We need to talk about it often, and we need to take a stand. So many children and women are vulnerable because they don't know how to speak up. Children don't know what sexual molestation is until years after it happened. How can we still prosecute the offender if we don't know it happened until years later? By then, the laws don't allow any room for prosecution.

Unfortunately, most children and women don't talk about it because they feel shame, and they feel like no one will believe them. Another reason why they don't say anything right away is because they don't want to expose the family member who was supposed to protect them, not hurt them.

It is much easier for a child to tell on a stranger than it is on a family member. Unfortunately, anything kept in secret has power over us. We cannot heal what we don't reveal. Silence and shame are a predator's favorite weapons. Their favorite words as they groom their victim are, "This will be our little secret," and, "Don't say anything because you will get in trouble if you say something." And because the child does not fully understand what is happening and what she/he should do, they keep silent.

We have got to rise up and speak up to heal and make a change. We desperately need a change in the current laws to bring hope and protection to all victims of sexual abuse.

Women get sexually molested and harassed as well, and the story is very similar to that of child molestation. It brings emotional pain, frustration, and anger against the offender. It also brings anger to family members when the offender is exposed. It's devastating.

"A 2000 person survey conducted by Growth From Knowledge stated that, nationwide, 81 percent of women and 43 percent of young men experience sexual harassment in their lifetime."[48]

According to inc.com, only 54 percent of women report workplace harassment.[49] Imagine the percentage of sexual harassment that happens in the home by a family member or a family friend that does not get reported. Most people who get sexually harassed or molested by a family member do not report the offender because they don't want to hurt their loved ones by exposing their offender.

This happened to me. From what I remember, I was about 4-6 years old when I was molested by a family friend. This sick man would isolate me and touch me inappropriately every time my parents were away. It happened several times, and I didn't know what to say or how to expose him because, at that age, I didn't know what sexual molestation was. When my parents found out about it, they immediately took action, and they were extremely angry.

Unfortunately, my parents didn't report it to the police. They just kicked him out and left things at that. You see, this is another offender who didn't get prosecuted. Do you think he stopped molesting children? Of course not. Who knows how many more children he continued molesting and how many more families he continued hurting.

At the age of seventeen, I was sexually harassed by an extended family member. He kept harassing me with sexual looks and comments that made me feel uncomfortable and unsafe in my own home. One night while I was asleep, I felt someone touching me and wanting to kiss me. I was paralyzed, and didn't know what to say or do. I pushed him away, and he left right away.

The next day, he came to me and told me that he wanted me and that he felt "bad" for trying to kiss me the night before. I felt disgusted by him and his actions. Then I told him to stop and to never do that again. I told him that he needed to respect the family and his wife (also an extended family member). I thought that his disgusting behavior was going to go away, but he kept harassing me every time he had an opportunity.

I didn't feel safe around him, so I told my mom that I wanted to move out and live with a friend of mine. She didn't want me to leave the house because I was too young to be out on my own. She kept asking why I wanted to leave, but I didn't want to say anything. Her mother's instincts kicked in and kept asking me more questions until I told her the truth. I told her that I wanted to leave because I didn't feel safe around him. I also asked my mom not to say anything to the rest of the family because I didn't want anyone to know.

It's very sad how our society has taught us for many generations to keep SILENT, and we automatically do it. My question is why? Why do we do this? Is it because of fear? Is it because of shame? Or is it because we don't want the family image to look dysfunctional according to our society?

When we choose to keep silent and not report any abuse, molestation, sexual harassment, or domestic violence, we automatically choose to be a part of the problem. Why, you may ask? Because when we don't speak up, we allow the problem to continue. Unfortunately, many of us choose to keep silent, all because of what people would say.

This is a sad truth, and we all need to speak up in order for the problem to get solved. In order for things to change, and in order for many victims to get true justice with our current laws, we all need to speak up and teach our children to speak up as soon as they get sexually molested or harassed.

Here are some things I found out that are very important to keep in mind and to use if you want our current laws to help and make an impact. Please pay attention to what I'm about to say, because these tips will help put a sexual predator in jail right away. Share them with anyone you know.

In order for the law to actually do justice, when children or women are touched inappropriately or harassed, you need to save or preserve the clothes you were wearing when the incident happened and immediately go to the police and file a report. We also need to save text messages or anything that can serve as physical evidence. If you have no physical evidence, the police will not press charges, and they will not be able to take your case to the court.

This is extremely frustrating to hear, because there are so many victims who keep silent, and when they finally gain enough straight to speak up and share what happened to them, they no longer have the physical evidence they need to back up their stories.

As you know, many victims hide their stories because they don't know how to share something that brings shame, confusion, and pain to them, and they keep it in private for many years. How are we going to bring justice if we don't speak up right away? Do not keep silent, because this will only benefit the offender.

So many families hide many horrible acts that happened to them or to their family members because of our current laws and also because of what "people would say." I'm pretty sure it's also because of their religious beliefs. Some families also keep silent for many years because they want to portray an impeccable image, according to our society.

This makes me sick to my stomach, and we must rise up and expose all evil acts and evil people. Silence is a killer. When we keep silent, we allow the offender to continue hurting others and continue getting away with their behavior. We must do everything we can to stop them.

When I shared with my mom what was happening, she got angry at the situation and at him, and she told everyone in the family. Of course, everyone got angry at him, but nobody reported it to the police. Nobody thought of that, nor even mentioned it.

One of the biggest reasons I kept silent was because I didn't want his kids to grow up without a father, because I grew up without a father. Because of my age and lack of knowledge, I didn't have the maturity to understand he could hurt others if he wasn't stopped. However, that's not a burden any child should have to carry. Unfortunately, he continued hurting others. I regret not exposing him right away. The emotional hurt and damage he created not just to me and to the other victims, but to the rest of the family, was devastating and hard to heal.

I also thought about the pain the news would cause his wife and her children. So I kept silent, and I thought that if I said no, he would stop harassing me. The only way these evil men stop harassing children and women is when they get exposed and prosecuted. I will repeat what I said earlier. The only way they get prosecuted is when you expose them right away. Don't wait! Gather all the physical evidence you can gather and report it to the police immediately.

Please remember that your evidence will expose the offender. This is the only way the offender will get stopped and prosecuted. Keep in mind that when you expose the offender, he will deny everything he did and he will blame the victim, turning himself into a victim. People who do these types of things are deceitful and evil. Don't be afraid to expose them. They will try to put fear on you by manipulating and gaslighting, but be strong and speak up.

If I had the power to prosecute and change the laws, I would. I would also make sure every child molester and any man who sexually harasses others paid for their actions, whether the sexual abuse was emotional or physical. This type of behavior must be prosecuted to the full extent of the law.

When there are no consequences or no strong laws for cases like this, sexual predators will always continue hurting others because they know that they won't get in trouble. They also know how to do it and how to get away with it. It is extremely frustrating and heartbreaking when we don't get justice for what has been done to us.

His wife knew everything, and she covered all his lies. I don't understand why someone would defend and cover such lies and evil actions for many years. My mind doesn't comprehend how a person can live with such lies and be in denial of reality. To defend and cover a sexual predator is beyond comprehension. It is very sad to see how much evil can exist in these types of people. No person in their right mind would ever do this or allow this to happen.

I cut all communication with these evil people forever. Even though I never ever want to see them again, I hope and pray they realize the damage they created and ask for forgiveness for the evil actions they did against me, my family members, and anyone else this man molested and harassed.

I don't know how people can sleep at night when they do all their evil acts, and how they live their lives one lie after another, pretending to be good people.

How can we create better laws that actually protect children and women from being molested, sexually harassed, and sexually abused? As far as I know, nobody is doing anything to change these laws, and it's hurting so many children and families.

The sad part is that there are so many men out there molesting and harassing children and women over and over again, and the current laws do not do justice. Many victims choose to stay silent because they know that our current laws are not strong enough to back them up.

Many victims I have spoken to regarding this subject told me this: "I don't want to say anything because I don't want to have to go through the memory again, and also because I don't want to hear the police say that they can't prosecute the offender because they don't have 'enough evidence.'" This is heartbreaking.

Also, when I spoke to a friend of mine who is a detective in southern California, he said, "I'm sorry. I wish I could help more. I believe your story and the stories of all the victims I talk to, but we can't do anything because we don't have physical evidence," and, "We cannot change the law—we only enforce it." This is very frustrating to hear, because there are many innocent children and women whose stories were marked "insufficient" for justice to be served.

The police have their hands tied, and they can't fully help, even if they wanted to. They are just doing what they can with what they have. This is why—again—I repeat, gather as much physical evidence as possible, because this will help you get the justice you deserve.

"Every 9 minutes, child protective services substantiates, or finds evidence for, a claim of child sexual abuse."[50] Every nine minutes. This is only in the United States. Imagine the percentage in other countries. This is devastating.

I hope that by me sharing my story, we can all come together and talk about our traumas and make it a purpose to do the work deep inside of us so we can start healing.

My forgiveness for this man is a work in progress. I hope he pays in full for everything he has done, not only to me, but to everyone else who he sexually harassed and molested. If God can bring justice, I pray he brings justice as soon as possible.

Why do I say this, and why am I sounding hateful towards him instead of sounding like I have healed and have forgiven him? After all, the whole purpose of my book is to heal our traumas, right? Well, as I mentioned earlier, my forgiveness for this man is still a work in progress. I also hate injustice.

Please know that forgiveness and healing are not something we do once, and then everything is perfect. The process of forgiveness and healing is a work in progress. Sometimes we can forgive things right away and move on, and sometimes we have to work on forgiving again and again until we can forgive fully.

Forgiveness is part of healing. We do need to forgive, but we don't need to be around the person who hurt us. I want you to know that it's okay to remove yourself from the people that hurt you, even if they are family. Sometimes your family is the people that hurt you the most.

Walk away from them. Don't stick around just because they are your "family." Do whatever it takes to protect yourself from anyone who hurts you, and create a safe environment that helps you heal your emotions. You have the right to do that. Work on forgiving at your own pace, and please remember to never keep silent. Stand up against anyone who abuses you.

When it comes to forgiving, there are different levels in the process of forgiveness. Sometimes you are going to forgive small offenses easily, but sometimes you are going to need to take time to forgive heavy and painful offenses. It is okay to take as much time as you need to process your pain in order to heal. In the case of sexual assault, it is not easy, and it's not a simple thing to do.

People have told me in the past that forgiveness is not for the benefit of the abuser—it's to help the victim with their wellbeing. There is a process for this type of healing and forgiving. I want you to take as long as you need. Don't let people tell you otherwise. People, and especially family, like to apply guilt when it comes to forgiveness.

Sometimes it's hard to forgive a person who has no remorse for his evil actions. When someone chooses to sexually molest or harass another human being, his actions are premeditated, and most offenders will always use fear, manipulation, and gaslighting to control the circumstance. They will always groom their victim before making their move. And, when they get exposed, they will lie and manipulate their way out of the situation. Don't let their behavior paralyze you.

The only way we can heal our traumas is by talking about them and letting go of any shame or fear. Fear paralyzes, and we cannot grow emotionally and spiritually if we allow fear to trap us and make us feel small. We are all created with gifts and powers to change our lives and the lives of others for the better. As we heal ourselves, we heal others.

Here are some resources you can keep, and reach out for help if you have been a victim or if you ever find yourself in any sexual harassment, sexual molestation, or sexual abuse situation.

- National Sexual Assault Hotline. Phone: 800-656-HOPE (4673) or chat online at online.rainn.org. It's free, confidential, and available 24/7.
- https://soundgirls.org/resources-for-sexual-harassment/
- National Domestic Violence Hotline. Phone: 800-799-SAFE (7233) or 800-787-3224 (TDD)
- https://www.cdc.gov/violenceprevention/sexualviolence/fastfact.html

10
MIRIAM

Toxic Relationships

Another example of a toxic relationship is Ana's friend Miriam and her husband. She fell in love with an "amazing, charming, and sweet" man, or at least she thought so. When they dated, he was attentive, romantic, and very loving and caring toward Miriam and her family. He gained Miriam and her family's trust right away.

A few months later, they decided to move in together. Miriam felt as though she was living her best life, but little by little that dream turned into a nightmare because he started being physically and verbally abusive towards her. His personality would go from being nice and calm to being angry, controlling, and verbally abusive.

Miriam was in love with him, and it was difficult for her to see or recognize that she was in an abusive relationship. Her culture didn't allow her to speak up and leave him. She continued in the relationship, even though she knew it was not the relationship she deserved. Miriam was afraid to speak and stand up for herself. She didn't know how to get out of the relationship because she didn't want to disturb the family dynamic.

After two years of living together, they got married because she felt pressured by her family. Her family didn't know his true personality. All he showed them was a sweet and charming personality. He was very good at hiding his dark side. Miriam was scared of him, so she hid what was happening.

He would threaten to kill her or her family if she said anything about the abuse, so she lived in fear, not knowing what to do or how to get out of the situation. She couldn't believe she was in another toxic relationship; she had gotten out of a similar relationship once before.

Miriam felt disappointed at herself for following the same patterns and not being able to change the outcome of her choices. She kept asking herself what was within her that was making her fall in love with abusive and narcissistic men.

She struggled in her marriage for several years, not knowing what to do. Her husband had addictions to gambling and pornography. He was also addicted to drugs and alcohol, which Miriam was not aware of until after they got married.

He had anger issues and exploded often, so Miriam was scared of him. She believed everything he would say to her every time he threatened her. Though she could not leave the relationship, she still wanted to protect her family, but didn't know how.

A few years went by, and as her children got old enough to understand the abusive relationship, her eldest son asked her to call the police and report everything. Her son told her, "If you don't report him to the police, I will kill him. I will no longer tolerate my dad abusing you emotionally and physically."

Miriam had to do something. Although she was scared, she still had to take action to protect her son. She had no choice but to stop the abusive and toxic pattern she was facing. The example she was giving to her children was not healthy, even though she thought she was doing the right thing to keep her family "safe."

How many times do we keep silent in abusive situations because we don't know what to do or we don't want to disrupt the "peace" or the family dynamic? Unfortunately, it is engrained in our minds to stay in toxic relationships. This is because we have been taught that if the relationship doesn't work out, somehow we are failures. Let me remind you that your emotional health is more important than anything else. Nothing in this life is worth it if you don't prioritize your emotional and physical health. Please keep in mind that no healthy partner will abuse you emotionally or physically.

Break down the lies of our society and break free from any type of abusive relationship you may find yourself in. Please hear me here. This advice also includes friendships, toxic family members, husbands, wives, boyfriends, girlfriends, bosses, employees, and coworkers. Essentially, if anybody abuses you, you must find a way to break free safely.

No good friend or family member, nor romantic partner, will manipulate you if they are healthy and if they truly love you. True and healthy relationships feel free and elevating. No one should isolate you or make you feel anxious, confused, gaslighted, or scared.

When a person who says they love you uses emotional abuse to manipulate you, they will also use anything to blame you and gaslight you so you feel confused. Then you end up doubting your reality. That is extremely toxic, and it is very important to do whatever you can to put a stop to those types of relationships.

Unfortunately, I also went through a few toxic relationships. Not to the same degree as my friend Miriam, but they were definitely toxic. In my last toxic relationship, to be more specific, I wasn't aware of it until a few years into the relationship. I felt emotionally drained, anxious, worried, and confused because I didn't know what I was dealing with.

I would find myself enabling him and fixing his problems so he would feel better and things would get back on track. Every time I came to the rescue, I thought everything would get solved and we would be ok.

Things would get better for a little while, but then they would go back to the same old patterns. And then again, I would go back and fix his problems. It was a life of codependency and emotional chaos. I didn't realize my life and energy were being consumed by negativity and unhealthy patterns that did not belong to me.

Believe it or not, this is abusive, emotionally speaking—abusive behavior is not only physical. Once I realized this truth, I started setting healthy boundaries for myself. He was dealing with difficult childhood trauma, and he would project his frustrations and negative attitude on me.

He would say that he loved me dearly, but he didn't know how to love me in a healthy way. He was too dependent on me and didn't know how to be emotionally healthy. He didn't know how to regulate his emotions.

It was not my responsibility to heal him or to fix his problems. It was his responsibility. He needed to look deep inside himself and take full responsibility for him to heal himself. We are all individually responsible for our own emotional and physical healing. We will never be successful at healing ourselves if we don't take personal responsibility.

When I needed help from him, he would not know how to connect with me to help me because all the focus was mainly on him. It was all about him and his victim behavior. He was comfortable playing the victim role because it worked for him during that time.

He didn't know he needed to heal his childhood trauma in order to stop his coping mechanisms. He also didn't know that by playing the victim, he wasn't growing. It didn't occur to him that by behaving the way he was behaving, he was hindering his potential and hurting our relationship and his relationships with others.

Every time we would go to counseling, he would cry or play the victim during our conversation, and that would make the counselor focus on him. We would finish the counseling session, and I would come out feeling confused and gaslighted. I knew there was a bigger problem, but I couldn't pinpoint it.

He would use excuses for his behavior and throw me under the bus every time it felt convenient to him. Every time he would do this, it would hurt me like a kick in the gut, yet I still didn't know how to recognize what I was dealing with, how to stop it, or how to walk away from it.

It was very hard for me to understand how a person with so much potential would live his life with so much negativity. He was constantly sabotaging himself and his potential.

His childhood and emotional traumas affected him and our relationship, and nothing was going to work until he took full responsibility to heal his emotional traumas and fix his unhealthy patterns.

I lived in this situation for several years. His unhealthy patterns and immature choices showed me exactly what I was dealing with. That's when I stood up for myself and took action to break free from the toxic relationship.

It was not easy, and it took a lot of me to break all the unhealthy habits. I was being toxic, too, by enabling his behavior. It was hard for me to say no and let him hit the wall.

I was used to coming to the rescue for everything and fixing both our problems. When I started saying no, part of me would feel guilty. I kept reminding myself that if I didn't create healthy boundaries for myself, I would never break free and heal my childhood traumas as well.

I started working on my emotional healing. First, I worked on learning how to stand up and speak up. Then I started to learn how to let go of unhealthy patterns and set healthy boundaries for myself.

After I started exercising my boundaries and making it clear to him that I would no longer allow anyone to manipulate me or emotionally abuse me, he started wanting to work on himself because he also wanted to be well and he didn't want to hurt me or our relationship.

He definitely made a positive change because he realized that no matter where he went, he needed to be responsible and think positively for the sake of his future. I also changed and created healthy boundaries for me, and I promised myself to never allow anyone to rob me of my inner peace and emotional wellbeing.

I can now say that I am very proud of him for making the changes that he made and for trying his best to become a healthy man. I am also very proud of me for standing up for myself and for setting healthy boundaries as I learned to heal. Anyone can become healthy emotionally and physically. They just have to want it more than others.

Please know that toxic relationships don't just happen out of nowhere. The majority of them happen because we carry childhood traumas. When we have unresolved emotional trauma, we attract more problems that create more trauma and pain.

My first experience with a toxic relationship began with my mother. My relationship with my mother was my first example of what it's like to live with a toxic person. Growing up, she would manipulate me, gaslight me and would make passive-aggressive comments.

I didn't know how to respond to that, so I developed coping mechanisms. I grew up thinking that enabling and pleasing people was the answer. I wasn't aware of the manipulation and gaslighting that was happening in my life. I didn't know what to call it.

It wasn't until I was thirty-five years old that I started learning how to identify gaslighting, enabling, codependency, passive-aggressive behaviors and the amount of damage that people-pleasing can cause. I had a big problem with people-pleasing and with setting healthy boundaries.

For many years as a child, and even as an adult, I had wanted my mother to accept me for who I was and to respect my mindset and personality. I was different from my family from a very early age. If I would point out any wrongdoing or something I didn't agree with, my mother and siblings would make jokes about me or practice name-calling.

My mother would also show favoritism between her own children. Even though she denied that behavior, it was easy to see. She would also make passive-aggressive comments when she was confronted about her behavior. I felt like they wanted to put me in a box and it had to be according to their own way of thinking, otherwise they would gossip about me and make negative comments about me.

They would criticize me, and they wanted me to accept their behavior. I developed a tendency to be a people-pleaser and an enabler of toxic behaviors. As I got old enough to make my own choices, I distanced myself from them, and I created my own path. I didn't want to be around controlling, critical, and manipulative people. I loved them but I didn't want to be around toxic behaviors.

As years went by and as I worked on my healing journey, I am able to see why people behave the way they behave. Many people operate in survival mode and also according to their own emotional traumas. Many people also lack wisdom and knowledge.

Without knowledge and wisdom, we parish. We stay stagnant.

As I see things with a lens of knowledge and wisdom now, I am able to see that my mother and siblings simply were not aware of their behavior. Especially my mother. She probably lived in survival mode as a mother. Maybe her experience of love was not healthy growing up and she tried to give love according to what she thought was love. I have love and compassion for her. I am sure she tried her best to be a good mother as most mothers do.

My relationship with my mother is much better now. I am able to set healthy boundaries for myself and she respects me and admires me for who I am. I am Thankful that she still in my life. She is a good person and a fun grandmother.

We can all change and become healthy emotionally speaking. Life is beautiful when we are able to heal our emotional and childhood traumas. It is not an easy journey when you decide to heal your childhood and emotional traumas but it is so rewarding and so beautiful when you become emotionally healthy.

No matter how hard we try, it will always be very difficult to have healthy relationships if we don't first work on our childhood traumas and coping mechanisms. Whatever experiences we had with our parents or family members, especially the toxic ones, we will end up with similar experiences with others. We fall into these types of relationships without even knowing it, repeating the familiar patterns because that is all we know.

When you are in a toxic relationship, it's very hard to get out of it or start making healthy changes. It's going to take hard work, and you are going to need to say no many times, but you need to be firm. You need to stay strong and say to yourself, "I will no longer allow toxic and unhealthy behaviors." You must keep your word with what you say you are going to do and stay consistent.

If the other person is willing to work with you and make healthy changes, that is gold. Allow them to take the steps they need to become healthy. I appreciated and was very thankful that my partner was willing to work on himself and made an effort to become healthy for us to have a healthy relationship, but I could not assume responsibility for him. In the end, he was the only one who could determine who he would become. My only responsibility was to heal me and know that the rest would take care of itself.

My hope and prayer for him was that he would continue working on himself so that he could become the best version of himself. All I wanted was peace and harmony in my life, even if I had to be on my own. My love and support were going to be there for him, as it always was, but with healthy boundaries.

Most people don't change, though. My advice to you is not to wait until the person changes, because you will be in for a rough journey, and the person may never change.

Now that I think about my past relationships, I realize that most of them were very similar to each other and very similar to my mother. This is very interesting, and I know why I was drawn to those types of relationships. My own childhood trauma kept me falling into the same toxic relationships. It is such an eye-opening lesson, and it brings so much freedom to my soul now that I can see everything with clarity. Remember, you cannot heal what you don't talk about.

This is why it is so important to heal our childhood traumas or any type of emotional trauma we may be carrying inside. For us to change our outcomes, we must first heal our pasts, otherwise you will repeat the same mistakes over and over again.

I kept repeating the same mistakes with my relationships. It wasn't just my romantic relationships; it was also my friendships. The friends I felt drawn to were jealous, backstabbers, gaslighters, and manipulators. I felt like I had to please them in order to keep the friendship. It was very difficult for me to understand it and keep up with it. A life like this is never sustainable. It is a very toxic life on so many levels. For a long time, my life felt so emotionally draining and exhausting.

I changed everything when I realized that no good friend does that, and no healthy relationship ever makes you feel confused, anxious, gaslighted, and manipulated. Once I had a clear vision of what I was dealing with and what I needed to do, I made a big change in my life to create a healthy environment for myself and the new relationships I would allow into my life.

This is why it is crucial to heal our childhood traumas and start our healing journeys. Life is very rewarding when we heal our childhood and emotional traumas. My life changed so much when I started setting healthy boundaries.

My life changed when I brought emotional healing to myself and my family. I brought healing to my past generations, which automatically brought healing to my present and future generations. I love the life I have created for myself, and I love the relationships I have now. They are loving, caring, nurturing, uplifting, and genuine. Be selective of your friendships and your relationships because they will determine the quality of your life.

Become aware of your emotional traumas and take action to start healing. Be brave and empower yourself to start your own healing journey. Your example will bring healing to those around you. Let's start an emotional healing domino effect!

Narcissism and Why Men Are More Likely to Have It vs. Women

As I worked through and studied many stories of women who were emotionally and physically abused by their partners, I discovered that narcissism can also be one of the reasons why men become abusive and have addictive behaviors.

Narcissism is a very difficult subject to talk about because it is not easy to understand. Most people don't talk about it, and if they do, they don't put in much effort to truly understand it. I am not a doctor and I am not a psychiatrist, but I would like to share some valuable information with you in hopes that we can bring more awareness to our behaviors

(Note: these explanations come from my own observations and studying people's behaviors and are not meant to serve as a replacement for talking to a psychologist or a professional. Please know that I'm just sharing the little bit I know. When it comes to narcissism, there is so much more that we need to know. I'm just scratching the surface here, and I do not claim to be an expert in this subject.)

Most psychologists and psychiatrists do not want to diagnose people with narcissistic traits because it takes a lot of deep medical research for them to give the full diagnosis. It is also difficult to diagnose a person because most narcissists will never admit that there is anything wrong with them.

Narcissistic traits are hard to pinpoint. However, here are some traits that are most common in people who may be narcissistic:

- They are self-focused.
- They seem perfect at first.
- They are charming.

- They lack empathy for others' emotions.
- They crave attention even if it is negative attention.
- They have an excessive need or admiration.
- They often isolate themselves socially.
- They are extremely sensitive to criticism.
- They are emotionally draining.
- They are manipulative.
- They cannot stand rejection.
- They have low self-esteem.
- They also have troubled relationships and problems at work.

Most people with narcissistic traits become narcissists because they use coping mechanisms to try to compensate for their childhood and emotional traumas.

When a child grows up in an environment that lacks love and safety, they will grow up insecure and with a deep need for attention. They also have anger issues, and they will get their anger out in different ways because they have trouble expressing their emotions. Due to childhood traumas and insecurities, a narcissistic person will try to compensate for what he didn't have growing up.

A child who grows up without emotional support and in an abusive environment becomes an emotionally broken adult. Emotional negligence will create a broken spirit in a child. It will also create anger and insecurities.

As the child becomes an adult, this individual will try to mask his pain through unhealthy behaviors such as anger, toxic masculinity, being controlling, being emotionally needy, and having addictions. There are so many ways a person will try to cope with his trauma.

Please know that I don't want to sound like I'm generalizing every case by what I just said. This doesn't mean that everyone who suffered as a child is a narcissist.

Fortunately, some children who were neglected or emotionally abused become amazing adults. Extremely loving, caring, emotionally healthy people and they actually become emotional healers. It all depends on the person and his or her ability to perceive and process their trauma. It depends on each individual's mindset and willingness to heal and become whole.

No matter what you went through as a child or as an adult, you can heal and restore your spirit. Don't be afraid to start your healing journey. It won't be easy as you start. You will have a lot of emotions running through you, making you doubt yourself, but keep working on your inner healing. It will be worth it because you will become a new you— beautiful, strong, and healthy, emotionally and physically.

You will discover your talents and potential, and you will see yourself the way God created you. You will see how much love you were designed with. You are love, and you were created with the ability to heal yourself from the inside out.

Our society has created an environment of trauma, confusion, ego, control, deep insecurities, war within ourselves, narcissism, and lack of love. In return, we have been dealing with toxic behaviors and some illnesses that can be treated or even cured by healing our emotional traumas.

The way parents raise their children and how they treat them is very important here. The parents' behavior will teach their children how to handle difficult situations as they go through life. We as parents have a big responsibility for our children's emotions and who they will become as adults. Remember that children learn from what we do and not from what we say. If a parent neglects a child's emotional wellbeing, a child will grow up with emotional trauma.

Also, if a parent spoils a child, the child will have an unhealthy behavior as well. They will grow up feeling entitled and disrespectful with no healthy boundaries. A lack of empathy is also common among adults who were spoiled as children. This is very dysfunctional.

When it comes to parenting, it is crucial for parents to teach their children healthy boundaries, love, attention, self-respect, respect for others, honor, confidence, responsibility, empathy, and, most importantly, how to regulate their emotions. Being emotionally present is very important as well.

Being emotionally present as a parent can make a big difference in a child's life and emotional wellbeing. When you are present and pay attention to your child's emotions, your child feels safe, loved, and cared for. They will also automatically feel secure and confident.

Nurture your children's emotional needs, and teach them how to regulate their emotions in a healthy way so when they become adults, they can build healthy habits. Allow them to think for themselves, and give them validation so that they can make responsible decisions on their own.

GENETIC DIFFERENCES IN MEN VS. WOMEN

According to an article I read by therecoveryvillage.com, narcissistic traits are more commonly found in men. "About 75% of people with narcissistic personality disorder are men."[51] This is mind-blowing. It intrigued me even more to continue doing my research, and I kept asking myself why this is and if there is a genetic reason behind it, or if it is a combination between genetics and environmental factors.

Let's go deeper and discover reasons why the percentage of narcissism is higher in men vs. women. Again, I repeat, I am not a doctor, and I am not an expert in biology and genetics, but this is my own hypothesis. Could it be a combination of genetics and environmental factors that are causing men to become narcissistic more often than women, or is it our society, as most people think?

What if the fact that male babies have fewer chances of survival due to lack of oxygen at birth is correlated with developmental delays and personality disorders in men as opposed to women? What if this statement is true? In order to get my question answered, I will need help from doctors and experts in genetics to test my hypothesis.

In the meantime, let's think about it. Girls have more chances of survival in the mother's womb vs. boys.[52] Did you know that? Let me tell you why. Boys naturally require more oxygen and more nutrients from their mothers compared to girls.[53] Not only that, but also at birth, boys have fewer chances of survival than girls.[54] This is a harsh reality.

When a baby suffers from lack of oxygen at birth, they will suffer from developmental delays and mental impairments.[55] This can happen to anyone, not just boys.

Babies who suffered from lack of oxygen at birth often get diagnosed with learning disabilities and behavioral disorders, poor memory, ADD, ADHD, depression, and anxiety, among other personality disorders.[56]

Narcissism is a personality disorder. According to the same article by therecoveryvillage.com, people who are narcissists, oftentimes, have been diagnosed with bipolar 1 disorder or bipolar 2 disorder.[57] People with personality disorders or mental disorders have obsessive and addictive behaviors that are toxic to their health and their relationships with others.

Unfortunately, many people struggle with this behavior and never do anything about it because they don't think there is anything wrong with them, and it is also because our society puts a stigma around it. It is very hard and emotionally draining for the family members caught in relationships with people who have narcissistic traits or behavioral problems.

I want you to think deeper here and become aware of your genetic makeup. I want you to know what to do to become healthy from the inside out, and ultimately be able to reverse any damage that was created in your mind and body from even before you were born.

Knowledge is power, and awareness is the beginning of your healing journey. If we learn about our genetic makeup and understand how it works, we can start working on bettering our health, and we can start taking steps towards a better future.

Genetics definitely plays a big role here. Scientifically speaking, as most of us know, the male provides one chromosome (either an X or a Y) and the female provides the other chromosome, which is always an X chromosome, to form a pair of chromosomes.[58] If both chromosomes are Xs, the baby is a girl, and if one chromosome is a Y and the other is an X, the baby is a boy.[59] There are always exceptions, like with some males having an extra X chromosome (XXY), which causes a genetic condition called Klinefelter Syndrome.[60] Different excess chromosomes create different genetic conditions.

Because females have two X chromosomes (XX), this gives them extra genetic material. Basically, they have a back-up chromosome that can compensate in case the other X chromosome has a bad mutation. This leaves her with at least one X chromosome that can be healthy.

Males, on the other hand, only have one X chromosome and one Y chromosome (XY), so they don't have a backup on some genes. A bad mutation on the X chromosome cannot be compensated by the Y chromosome.

Why am I talking about this, and why does the X chromosome sound more important than the Y chromosome? Let me explain it things a little better. The X chromosome carries more genetic material in humans; it has about 155 million base pairs, and a Y chromosome only carries about 59 million base pairs.[61] It also contains more genes (about 1000 genes) compared to the Y chromosome, but on the other hand, a Y chromosome contains fewer than 80 genes.[62] Basically, a X chromosome is more than five times larger than the Y chromosome.

This may sound unfair for men, but unfortunately, it is very true. Sorry, gentlemen, I really do feel for you. Please know that God never makes mistakes. If he made you with only one X chromosome, it's because that was enough for him to equip you with everything you need. If you lack anything, there are always ways to better your health.

Genetics is not the only thing that causes behavioral problems. We also must add other elements such as the environment in which the child grew up, their parents' beliefs, society's expectations, and the way the mother took care of herself during the pregnancy.

Think about it. When the woman doesn't take care of herself during the pregnancy, there are health consequences for the child. If women take care of themselves during pregnancy, we could have healthier babies. The right exercises, eating healthy, and not smoking or drinking all help us to have healthier babies. If our behavior brings negative consequences, could our changed behavior bring about positive changes in our lives? I believe we can reverse the way that our genes are expressed in our bodies.

It is important to understand each of our genetic makeups and what we can do to build healthier mindsets. I am bringing awareness so we can all see how amazing our human DNA is and how powerful we are. We have the power to change our outcomes and heal ourselves from the inside out.

Nothing that meant to hurt you, whether it was emotionally or physically, can keep you from healing and becoming a new and healthy you. If you, as a child, grew up in a harsh environment, you can heal your body and mind from emotional trauma. It must be work that comes from within you. I cannot heal you. Nobody else can heal you either. Your healing comes from within. You have the power to heal yourself from the inside out. Your mind is powerful. As Dr. Amen says in his book title, "Change your brain, Change your Life."[63]

Our bodies and minds are amazing at healing us when we do the work. We can definitely regenerate our cells and rewire our brains. Please understand that it will take hard work as you let go of old programing to adopt the new healthy programing. It takes consistency, and most importantly, it takes AWARENESS.

Awareness is everything! When you become aware, you can change anything. AWARENESS is the beginning of your healing journey. It is the wisdom we were all born with. Become aware and take action. Heal your traumas and become emotionally healthy and free. I hope with all my heart that my words inspire you to start your healing journey.

PART IV
Your Next Steps

11

FINDING YOUR INNER POWER

Do the Mirror Work

Do the mirror work—what do I mean by that? When you want to heal your emotional traumas, become a new you, and change old habits and toxic behaviors, you must be honest and transparent with yourself. The mirror doesn't lie.

When you see yourself in front of the mirror, you can see the real you. Your eyes reveal what is inside of you; your eyes will speak for your soul. If you are not happy or don't accept yourself, you will not like what you see.

You will know it, and you will either have the courage to work on it or you'll mask it. Every time you choose to not be honest with yourself and mask your trauma, you choose to hinder your potential.

When you see yourself in front of the mirror, everything you have inside of you comes out, whether it is good or bad. It is very important to remember that as you do the mirror work, you talk to yourself in front of the mirror.

Ask yourself questions. Talk about your childhood traumas, your pain, your dreams, your fears, your insecurities, your disappointments, what you are proud of, and your happy moments. Everything!

Forgive yourself and work on forgiving those who hurt you. Give yourself grace and love yourself as you work on becoming a better and healthier you. You will feel lighter and freer, emotionally and physically.

As you do this deep, emotional work, please be patient with yourself because it is not an easy process or a one-time thing. It's a lifetime commitment, a journey, and it is worth it.

Don't feel discouraged if it takes you years to fully heal, especially when it comes to forgiving others. Healing our traumas takes time, and we are all different. Allow yourself to heal at your own pace.

As you look at yourself in the mirror and do the work, I hope you do. I am not talking about physical features; I am talking about your inner spirit, your soul and beliefs about yourself, your deep wounds.

Don't just look at yourself in front of the mirror. Talk to yourself in front of the mirror. Listen to your voice. Be honest and transparent about your feelings and emotions.

Pour out all the negative, sad, and angry emotions, anything you have. Once you allow yourself to process all the emotions, elevate yourself with positive words. Tell yourself you are worthy of receiving healing. You are loved. There is no fear in love. When you finally love yourself, you will feel safe.

When you feel safe, your brain will think clearly and it automatically becomes creative. You will grow and see your true purpose. This safety will allow you to connect your heart and brain. When your heart and brain are in tune with each other, there is harmony that radiates from within.

As you speak to yourself in front of the mirror, tell yourself you are safe. You are beautiful inside and out. You are powerful when you believe in yourself. You are a gift to the world. You are wise when you know who you are. You are blessed, and you are a blessing.

Allow yourself to receive the healing you need. Give yourself permission to feel again. Allow yourself to dream and trust in yourself. Be at peace with whom you are. Feel proud of yourself and your journey, because you are an amazing human being. You are LOVED!

The Story of the Golden Buddha

I'd love to share with you one of my favorite stories, a very famous story from Thailand.

The story says that many years ago in Ayutthaya, an ancient city in Thailand, there was a temple with many statues, but one in particular stood out because of its size. Nobody knew its actual value because it was covered in mud, concrete, and colored glass. This statue was covered by the monks to protect it from thieves and the invading armies.

For many years, this statue was seen as a mud statue with no value, and people forgot what the statue was actually made of. Then one day, a young monk who was meditating at the base of the Buddha statue was curious and started scraping it off, bit by bit. Little did he know that the statue was made of gold. Real gold!

The curious monk couldn't believe his eyes! He was so excited, and he ran back to the village to tell everyone that the statue was made of gold.

They all ran towards the Buddha statue and started cleaning and removing all the mud, concrete, and glass until they revealed its true value.

This Buddha statue is currently one of the tallest statues in the world. It is also known as the Great Buddha of Thailand.

The moral of the story:

You see, in life, each of us is the golden Buddha. Inside and outside, we are golden. God created us golden, beautiful, and with many talents. We are born knowing love and trusting in ourselves, full of confidence, happy and joyful. But as we go through trials in life, and as we are taught by society how to live, how to dress, how to eat, and even what to believe, we start putting barriers on ourselves. We start feeling diminished and confused. We start blocking our minds. We lose value, and we lose our vision.

As we go through life's challenges, we start believing that we are the stone Buddha and not the golden Buddha.

Then something or someone comes along and helps us crack the casing of mud and concrete that we created over the years in our lives to protect us from the outside world. We finally get to look inside and see the gold within us. We start seeing the true beauty and true value within us.

Once we see a little bit of gold, we keep digging until all our gold shines through. Then we realize that the old mindsets we had no longer have power over us because we have been awakened to our true potential.

Once you can see your true potential, the sky is the limit, and nothing and no one has power over you besides what you allow.

You are that golden Buddha! Each of us are a golden Buddha! Don't you ever forget that, my friend.

Get up, dust yourself off, and become the person you were meant to be in this beautiful world. Our world needs emotionally healed people. Our world needs brave people who are willing to be raw with their emotions and take action to transform themselves into healthy and loving human beings.

ACKNOWLEDGMENTS

I would like to thank God for giving me the wisdom, the words to speak, and the strength to push forward when I felt like giving up.

I would also like to thank all my friends who encouraged me to write this book. I really appreciate my friends who were truly there for me and who gave me emotional support during difficult times.

On the professional side, I would like to thank Kary Oberbrunner and the gift he has to encourage and empower people to write their stories. Before I decided to write a book, I would listen to him on social media, and his kind spirit encouraged me to write my book. I knew I needed to write my book and when I saw Kary talking about his books and his ministry growing up, I felt encouraged to right my story and turn it into a book.

Thank you, everyone, from the bottom of my heart.

NOTES

1. "The Science of Early Childhood Development (InBrief)." Center on the Developing Child. Retrieved from www.developingchild.harvard.edu.2007. https://developingchild.harvard.edu/resources/inbrief-science-of-ecd/.
2. Ibid
3. Ibid
4. Fraga, Juli. "Do the First 7 Years of Life Really Mean Everything?" Healthline. December 21, 2017. https:// www.healthline.com/health/parenting/first-seven-years-of-childhood.
5. "'It's easier to build strong children than to repair broken men.' Frederick Douglass – Education." Teach Different. https://teachdifferent.com/podcast/

its-easier-to-build-strong-children-than-to-repair-broken-men-teach-different-with-frederick-douglass-education/.

6 Allen, Suzanne. "Metabolic Acidosis: Causes, Symptoms & Treatments." Healthline. March 22, 2022. https:// www.healthline.com/health/acidosis.

7 "Get Enough Sleep." Office of Disease Prevention and Health Promotion. Last updated July 15, 2022. https:// health.gov/myhealthfinder/healthy-living/mental-health-and-relationships/get-enough-sleep#:~:text=How%20much%20sleep%20do%20I,reste d%20when%20you%20wake%20up.

8 Ibid

9 Parker, Hilary. "Physical Side Effects of Oversleeping." WebMD. January 15, 2022. https://www.webmd.com/sleep-disorders/physical-side-effects-oversleeping.

10 Jabr, Ferris. "Does Thinking Really Hard Burn More Calories?" Scientific American. July 18, 2012. https:// www.scientificamerican.com/article/thinking-hard-calories/.

11 Gomez-Pinilla, Fernando. "Brain foods: the effects of nutrients on brain function." National Library of Medicine. Nat Rev Neurosci 2008 Jul, 9(7): 568-578. doi: 10.1038/ nrn2421.

12 Amen MD, Daniel. "Brain Food." brainMD. October 6, 2020. https://brainmd.com/blog/best-memory-boosting-foods/.

13 "Omega-3 and dementia." Alzheimer's Society. https:// www.alzheimers.org.uk/about-dementia/risk-factors-and-prevention/omega-3-and-dementia#:~:text=Omega%2D3%20is%20important%20for,important%20process%20for%20brain%20function.

14 Delaney. "Nourish Your Body and Mind with The Mediterranean Diet." Acupuncture Connections. April 25, 2023. https://acupunctureconnections.com/nourish-your-body-and-mind-with-the-mediterranean-diet/.

15 Fischetti, Mark and Jen Christiansen. "Our Bodies Replace Billions of Cells Every Day." Scientific American. April 1, 2021. https://www.scientificamerican.com/article/our-bodies-replace-billions-of-cells-every-day/.

16 Dispenza, Joe. "New Studies Continuously Point to the Efficacy of Meditation." DrJoeDispenza.com. May 9, 2019. https://drjoedispenza.com/blogs/dr-joes-blog/new-studies-continuously-point-to-the-efficacy-of-meditation.

[17] "Goodness Weekly 11.7.22." Sunset Ridge Collective. November 7, 2022. https://sunsetridgecollective.org/goodness-weekly/2ztmlnp8tgx553h.

[18] "The Brain-Gut Connection." Johns Hopkins Medicine. Accessed November 22, 2022. www.hopkinsmedicine.org/health/wellness-and-prevention/the-brain-gut-connection.

[19] Li, Yuanyuan, et al. "The Role of Microbiome in Insomnia, Circadian Disturbance and Depression." National Library of Medicine. Front Psychiatry 9: 669 (2018). doi: 10.3389/fpsyt.2018.00669.

[20] Zhang, Yu-Jie, et al. "Impacts of Gut Bacteria on Human Health and Diseases." National Library of Medicine. Int J Mol Sci 16(4): 7493-7519 (2015). doi: 10.3390/ijms16047493; Lv, Zhiming, et al. "The Interaction Between Viruses and Intestinal Microbiota: A Review." National Library of Medicine. Curr Microbio 78(10): 3597-3608 (2021). doi: 10.1007/s00284-021-02623-5; Pathak MD, Neha. "How Your Gut Health Affects Your Whole Body." WebMD. January 28, 2023. https://www.webmd.com/digestive-disorders/ss/slideshow-how-gut-health-affects-whole-body.

21 "Disorders of the Immune System." Johns Hopkins Medicine. Accessed November 22, 2022. https://www.hopkinsmedicine.org/health/conditions-and-diseases/disorders-of-the-immune-system.

22 Li, Yangping, et al. "Healthy lifestyle and life expectancy free of cancer, cardiovascular disease, and type 2: prospective cohort study." Thebmj. BMJ 2020;368:l6669. doi: https://www.bmj.com/content/368/bmj.l6669.

23 Galvin, Gaby. "The U.S. Obesity Rate Now Tops 40%." U.S. News. February 27, 2020. https://www.usnews.com/news/healthiest-communities/articles/2020-02-27/us-obesity-rate-passes-40-percent.

24 GBD 2017 Diet Collaborators. "Health effects of dietary risks in 195 countries, 1990-2017: a systematic analysis for the Global Burden of Disease Study 2017." The Lancet. Vol 393, issue 10184 (2019) P1958-1972. doi: https://doi.org/10.1016/S0140-6736(19)30041-8.

25 Bawa, A.S., K.R. Anilakumar. "Genetically modified foods: safety, risks and public concerns—a review." National Library of Medicine. J Food Sci Technol 50(6): 1035-1046 (2013). doi: 10.1007/s13197-012-0899-1.

26 "Herbicides and GMO crops." Ewg.org. https://www.ewg.org/herbicides-and-gmo-crops.

27 Ibid

28 Peltzer, Sally and Alex Douglas. "Movement of herbicides in the environment." Updated October 25, 2022. https://www.agric.wa.gov.au/herbicides/herbicides?page=0%2C4.

29 "ADHD Natural Treatments and Remedies Directory." WebMD. https://www.webmd.com/add-adhd/adhd-natural-treatments-remedies-directory; Sosnoski PhD, Karen. "The Best Meditation Strategies for ADHD." PsychCentral. March 21, 2022. https:// psychcentral.com/adhd/adhd-meditation.

30 "Sugar & ADHD: Does Sugar Make ADHD Symptoms Worse?" Drake Institute of Neurophysical Medicine. https://www.drakeinstitute.com/sugar-consumption-and-adhd#:~:text=Some%20sweeteners%2C%20like%20Aspartame%20and,can%20also%20disrupt%20brain%20functioning; the mini adhd coach. "Optimizing Your Diet for ADHD: Recommended Foods and Foods to Avoid." Theminiadhdcoach.com. October 27, 2022. https://www.theminiadhdcoach.com/living-with-adhd/adhd-diet.

31 the mini adhd coach. "Optimizing Your Diet for ADHD: Recommended Foods and Foods to Avoid." Theminiadhdcoach.com. October 27, 2022. https://

www.theminiadhdcoach.com/living-with-adhd/adhd-diet.

32 Hub staff report. "Meditation effective in treating anxiety, depression, Hopkins research suggests." Hub. January 8, 2014. https://hub.jhu.edu/2014/01/08/meditate-to-reduce-depression/.

33 BW Online Bureau. "20 Minutes' Meditation Is Equivalent To 4-5 Hours Of Deep Sleep, Say Experts At ASSOCHAM's 'Illness To Wellness' Series." BW Education. December 31, 2020. http://bweducation.businessworld.in/article/20-Minutes-Meditation-Is-Equivalent-To-4-5-Hours-Of-Deep-Sleep-Say-Experts-At-ASSOCHAM-s-Illness-To-Wellness-Series/31-12-2020-360099/.

34 "The moment you change your perception is the moment you rewrite the chemistry of your body." Quotefancy.com. https://quotefancy.com/quote/1519510/Bruce-H-Lipton-The-moment-you-change-your-perception-is-the-moment-you-rewrite-the.

35 "Emotional Pain: Your Thoughts Can Make You Sick." The Roaming Mind. January 16, 2019. https://theroamingmind.com/2019/01/16/surviving-pain-thoughts-make-sick/.

36 Hassennally, Jaleela. "The Importance of a Freedom of Information Act in Mauritius." Transparency Mauritius. https://www.transparencymauritius.org/wp-content/uploads/2016/03/UPD-FOIA-SPEECH.pdf.

37 Seales, Rebecca. "Let's save Maya Angelou from fake quotes." BBC. November 13, 2017. https://www.bbc.com/news/41913640.

38 Chapman, Gary. "What are the 5 Love Languages?" 5lovelanguages.com. https://5lovelanguages.com/store/what-are-the-5-love-languages.

39 "The Quote Archive." Tiny Buddha. https://tinybuddha.com/wisdom-quotes/either-get-bitter-get-better/.

40 "How Common is Divorce and What are the Reasons?" YourDivorceQuestions.org. https://yourdivorcequestions.org/how-common-is-divorce/.

41 Lang, Katharine. "Ultra-processed foods may increase depression risk, long-termstudy shows." Medical News Today. May 22, 2023. https://www.medicalnewstoday.com/articles/ultra-processed-foods-may-increase-depression-risk-long-term-study- shows#1.

42 WebMD Editorial Contributors. "Depression vs. Anxiety: Which One Do I Have?" WebMD. January

43 Ibid

44 Dispenza, Joe. *You Are the Placebo: Making Your Mind Matter*. New York, NY: Hay House Inc., 2014.

45 "Victims of Sexual Violence: Statistics." RAINN. https://www.rainn.org/statistics/victims-sexual-violence.

46 "Children and Teens: Statistics." RAINN. https://www.rainn.org/statistics/children-and-teens.

47 "Department of Family Services – Domestic and Sexual Violence Services." Fairfax County Virginia. https://www.fairfaxcounty.gov/familyservices/domestic-sexual-violence/sexual-violence/ statistics.

48 "Sexual Harassment Statistics." Matthew & George Attorneys at Law. https://www.caemployeelawyer.com/sexualharassment-statistics/.

49 Zetlin, Minda. "54 Percent of Women Report Workplace Harassment. How Is Your Company Responding?" Inc.com. https://www.inc.com/magazine/201804/minda-zetlin/sexual-harassment-workplace-policy-metoo.html.

Starts with: "18, 2023. https://www.webmd.com/depression/depression-or-anxiety."

50 "Children and Teens: Statistics." RAINN. https://www.rainn.org/statistics/children-and-teens.

51 The Recovery Village. "Narcissistic Personality Disorder Statistics." The Recovery Village Drug and Alcohol Rehab. Updated May 8, 2023. https://www.therecoveryvillage.com/mental-health/narcissistic-personality-disorder/npd-statistics/.

52 Roberts, Claire, et al. "Why are girl babies winning in the battle for survival?" The University of Adelaide. May 28, 2014. https://www.adelaide.edu.au/news/news70802.html.

53 "Designing individual treatment plans and encouraging pregnant women to make lifestyle changes based upon the sex of their unborn babies could have lifelong health benefits for their children." April 26, 2022. https://www.joh.cam.ac.uk/boys-are-more-demanding-girls-they-are-born-according-scientists#:~:text=Male%20baby%20pregnancies%20are%20more,the%20fetus%20grow%20and%20develop.

54 Pongou, Roland. "Why Is Infant Mortality Higher in Boys Than in Girls? A New Hypothesis Based on Preconception Environment and Evidence From a Large Sample of Twins." Duke University Press. Demography 50 (2): 421-444 (2013). doi: https://doi.org/10.1007/s13524-012-0161-5.

55 Beam Legal Team. "Can Lack of Oxygen During Birth Cause Development Delays?" Beam Legal Team. September 15, 2017. https://www.beamlegalteam.com/blog/2017/september/can-lack-of-oxygen-during-birth-cause-development/.

56 Raab, Susanne. "Long Term Effects of Birth Asphyxia." Birth Injury Lawyers Alliance. https://www.bila.ca/birth-injuries/hypoxic-ischemic-encephalopathy-hie/effects-asphyxia/#:~:text=Infants%20who%20experience%20mild%20or,cerebral%20palsy%2C%20and%20developmental%20delays; Dzikiene, Renata, et al. "Long-Term Outcomes of Perinatal Hypoxia and Asphyxia at an Early School Age." National Library of Medicine. Medicina (Kaunas) 57(9): 988 (2021). doi: 10.3390/medicina57090988; Sissons, Beth. "What are the causes of birth asphyxia?" MedicalNewsToday. October 23, 2020. https://www.medicalnewstoday.com/articles/birth-asphyxia#effects; Giannopoulou, I., et al. "Perinatal hypoxia as a risk factor for psychpathology later in life: the role of dopamine and neurotropins." Springer Link. Hormones 17, 25–32 (2018). https://doi.org/10.1007/s42000-018-0007-7.

57 The Recovery Village. "Narcissistic Personality Disorder Statistics." The Recovery Village Drug

and Alcohol Rehab. Updated May 8, 2023. https://www.therecoveryvillage.com/mental-health/narcissistic-personality-disorder/npd-statistics/.

[58] Vorvick MD, Linda J., et al. "Chromosome." MedlinePlus. May 3, 2021. https://medlineplus.gov/ency/article/ 002327.htm.

[59] Ibid

[60] WebMD Editorial Contributors. "Klinefelter Syndrome (XXY Syndrome)." WebMD. September 22, 2021. https:// www.webmd.com/men/klinefelter-syndrome.

[61] "Write the differences between the sex chromosomes of man and sex chromosomes of woman." Toppr. September 5, 2022. https://www.toppr.com/ask/en-us/question/write-the-differences-between-the-sex-chromosomes-of-man-and-sex-chromosomes-of-woman/.

[62] Pfizer Staff. "Inside the X-(Chromosome) Files." Pfizer. https://www.pfizer.com/news/articles/inside_the_x_chromosome_files.

[63] Amen MD, Daniel G. "Change Your Brain, Change Your Life." Las Vegas, NV: Harmony, 2015.

ABOUT THE AUTHOR

Lily Robinson was born in Mexico and moved to the United States at the age of sixteen. She lived in Orange County from the age of sixteen to the age of twenty-three and then she moved to Hawaii, where she got married and had her three beautiful children.

She is a mother, daughter, sister, friend, and a businesswoman. Through her life experiences and her entrepreneurial endeavors, Lily's empathic nature has led her to meet and help others work through their emotional traumas and ultimately heal and become the best version of themselves. Her love, personal trials and compassion for others has led her to write this book to bring hope and healing to everyone who reads it.

:simple-instagram: @lilyrobinson_author_lifecoach

:simple-facebook: facebook.com/lilian17robinson

:simple-linkedin: lily-robinson-21788472

:simple-tiktok: tiktok.com/lilyrobinson777

:simple-youtube: youtube.com/@07LilyR

CONNECT WITH LILY ROBINSON

www.ingramcontent.com/pod-product-compliance
Lightning Source LLC
Chambersburg PA
CBHW050246010526
44107CB00003B/199